D0552321

Ibiza
and Formentera

Berlitz®
Ibiza
and Formentera

Text: Jack Altman
Editor: Richard Wallis
Photography: Jack Altman pages 5, 6, 10, 19,
22, 28, 33, 36, 39, 43, 46, 62, 66, 79, 81, 84;
Jon Davison pages 3, 4, 9, 15, 16, 24, 27, 51, 53,
54, 57, 59 (bottom), 61, 69, 75, 76, 88
Cover photograph: Apa/Bill Wassman
Layout: Media Content Marketing, Inc.
Cartography: Ortelius Design
Managing Editor: Tony Halliday

Ninth Edition 2004 (Reprinted 2004)

CONTACTING THE EDITORS
Every effort has been made to provide accurate information in this publication, but
changes are inevitable. The publisher cannot be responsible for any resulting loss,
inconvenience or injury. We would appreciate it if readers would call our attention
to any errors or outdated information by contacting Berlitz Publishing, PO Box 7910,
London SE1 1WE, England. Fax: (44) 20 7403 0290;
e-mail: berlitz@apaguide.co.uk; www.berlitzpublishing.com

Printed in Singapore by Insight Print Services (Pte) Ltd, 38 Joo Koon Road, Singapore
628990. Tel: (65) 6865-1600. Fax: (65) 6861-6438

050/409 RP

CONTENTS

● A  in the text denotes a highly recommended sight

Ibiza
and Formentera

THE ISLANDS AND THEIR PEOPLE

The miracle of Ibiza is that its continuing success, first with an élite then with package-holiday visitors, has not hurt its legitimate claim to being, simply, a beautiful island. While some come just to have fun all day and all night, the island has many other things to offer. Together with its little neighbour, Formentera, Ibiza – or Eivissa, to give it its local name – belongs to Spain's semi-autonomous province of the Balearic Islands (Islas Baleares). The province, which includes Mallorca and Menorca, faces Spain's east coast, between Barcelona and Valencia.

Ibiza's coastline varies, with long curving stretches of fine sand (great both for beach parties and family activities) alternating with smaller, secluded coves and fjord-like inlets which offer somewhat more seclusion. Coastal waters are kept clean by stringently enforced anti-pollution laws.

The resort towns have every imaginable kind of disco and bar, each trying to rise higher on the island's own seismic scale of outrageous extravagance. Yet it is always possible to escape to a classic Mediterranean landscape (now well protected by environmental laws) abundant in groves of olives, figs, almonds, junipers, palms (to remind us that North Africa is closer than Barcelona) and – above all – shady pine woods. The profusion of these trees prompted the Greeks to call Ibiza and Formentera the 'Isles of Pines', a name the Spanish retained as *Islas Pitiusas*. For a perfect view of this landscape as well as of the Spanish mainland, drive up to the top of Mount Sa Talaia, which at 475 m (1,558 ft) is the island's highest spot.

Partygoers too exhausted to ramble along clifftop paths or through the wooded wilderness of the interior can hunker down with more peaceful people in one of the many old inland villages that have retained their traditional charm. Here, more than in the resorts, you will hear people speaking Ibicenco, which is the island variation of Catalan, now the official language. In a bar or café across from a gleaming white church and a couple of shops selling straw baskets and terracotta vases, you can sip *hierbas,* an aromatic liqueur distilled from local herbs.

On the Right Track

The islanders' language, Ibicenco, reflects their multiple origins. It has connections with Latin (from the Romans), Arabic (from North African settlers) but mostly Catalan, also Romance-based (from the rulers who effected the Christian reconquest of the island in the 13th century, and held onto it). Place names are usually signposted in Ibicenco rather than Castilian Spanish, for example, Eivissa (Ibiza) or Sant Antoni (San Antonio).

The following list of useful terms should help keep you on the right track. Castilian Spanish words are provided with their local Ibicenco equivalents.

English	Castilian/Ibicenco	English	Castilian/Ibicenco
palace	*palacio/palau*	quarter	*barrio/barri*
boulevard	*paseo/passeig*	river	*río/riu*
bridge	*puente/pont*	square	*plaza/plaça*
street	*calle/carrer*	cape	*cabo/cap*
cave	*cueva/cova*	church	*iglesia/església*
road	*carretera/*	harbour	*puerto/port*
	carretera	beach	*playa/platja*
avenue	*avenida/avinguda*	town hall	*ayuntamiento/*
	or vía/via		*ajuntament*

For many people, the ideal refuge from the bustle of Ibiza is its diminutive island neighbour to the south, Formentera. Ibiza is small, with an area of 572 sq km (220 sq miles) and 80,000 residents, but Formentera is really tiny. It has a population of barely 5,000 living on just 82 sq km (32 sq miles). It lies only one hour away by ferry and 25 minutes by hydrofoil. Painters love it. Poorer than Ibiza, it holds on more firmly to its traditions. The peasant women still wear black; old stone housing is restored from generation to genera-

Far from the madding crowd, a peaceful mountain home in Serra de la Mala Costa.

tion rather than razed and replaced by concrete. Its beaches are less accessible and less crowded. Farther afield, if you have access to a boat, you will find even more idyllically secluded beaches on other, much tinier isles, some of them scarcely more than a rocky outcrop topped by a tree or two, particularly off Ibiza's wilder west coast.

This is not to say that you should spend your whole time running away from what gives Ibiza its distinctive character. Ibiza remains very much an island where people come to have fun. However, it also lures some of the modest successors to the hippies of the 1960s who gave Ibiza its modern fame – or notoriety, depending on your point of view. Wealthy visitors have added swimming pools and tennis courts to tastefully restored farmhouses *(fincas)*. They have also built in the inland hills their own handsome white villas in the traditional cubic style that was introduced centuries ago by Arab landowners.

Resolutely democratic, Ibiza welcomes all sorts to its bars and discos and to the midnight-to-dawn beach raves that make no distinction between penniless and privileged. It also has a strong gay community. The island's freewheeling attitude to life is epitomised by the name given to its own designer fashion and hairstyles – 'Ad Lib' – coined in the heady 1960s and still going strong. As *the* place to be for nightlife, which reaches a crescendo from around 3am with no diminuendo till dawn, Ibiza Town (Eivissa) has to

Traditional transport near Sant Lorenç de Balàfia in the northeast of the island.

compete with equally boisterous satellites out at Sant Antoni and Santa Eulària, conveniently linked by an all-night 'Discobus' shuttle service, running every 30 minutes.

In Eivissa the cathedral, convents and museums inside the walled citadel of Dalt Vila rise above the bars and bistros lining La Marine on the harbourside, and the boutiques and vegetable market in the narrow streets of La Penya. The east-coast resort of Santa Eulària (Santa Eulalia in Castilian) adds 'del Riu' to its name in honour of the island's only river (running just west of the town centre) and has an imposing fortress-church overlooking the attractive harbour and marina. Busiest of the tourist towns is the ever-growing Sant Antoni (San Antonio in Castilian), with high-rise hotels mushrooming up around a magnificent bay and a revered parish church attracting pilgrims to the heart of the town centre.

Those keen on archaeology can seek out the prehistoric monoliths near Santa Eulària or on Formentera. There are also early Carthaginian sites: the Grotto of Es Cuieram north of Sant Vicent and Eivissa's necropolis of Puig des Molins. Or you can simply study the ancient relics in the capital's two well-stocked archaeology museums.

The Mediterranean climate means there are no great extremes of temperature. The heat of high summer is usually tempered by sea breezes and days are generally warm throughout the year, although fierce winter storms are not uncommon. The island's agriculture thrives on its exceptional underground water resources. Vegetables and fruit – olives, apricots, figs, grapes, almonds, oranges and lemons galore – arrive fresh on your table. In addition to the local seafood, pork and lamb, prepared in the traditional manner with the island's fresh herbs, can be a savoury delight. By night or day, Ibiza is a place for hedonists.

A BRIEF HISTORY

Circles of stone megaliths dating back to 1600 BC are the earliest traces of human life on Ibiza and Formentera. Two monumental sites were probably funerary in origin. The better preserved of these is located on Formentera at Ca Na Costa. The other has been excavated on a coastal Ibiza hillside at Cap d'Es Librell, south of Santa Eulària. Rock paintings from 800 BC have been found at Ses Fontanelles, near Sant Antoni.

Little else is known of Ibiza's prehistoric inhabitants. The Mediterranean world appears to have ignored the island until its freshwater springs made it a popular stopover for Phoenician seamen plying the route between the European mainland and North Africa.

The Carthaginians

Sailing from their great ports of Tyre and Sidon (modern Lebanon's Soûr and Saïda), the enterprising Phoenician traders founded the city of Carthage on the Tunisian coast in the 9th century BC. Two hundred years later they set up colonies on Ibiza, whose name first appeared as *Yb'sim* on Phoenician-Carthaginian coins. This became *Ebysos* to the Greeks, *Ebusus* to the Romans and *Yebisah* to later Arab settlers. At the etymological root of the name is the deity Bes, a jolly, bearded dwarf whom the Phoenicians shared with the ancient Egyptians, and whose music drowned out the rage of the angry spirits.

In 654 BC the Carthaginian colonists built the hilltop acropolis of Ereso, which was to become today's Ibiza Town. From their strongholds in North Africa, and Cádiz on the Spanish mainland, they challenged the Roman Empire for domination of the Mediterranean region. Ibiza's contribution to the

Carthaginians' war effort came from its lead mines (active until the 20th century), which provided ammunition for the great general Hannibal in his epic battles with the Romans. The colonists' commercial interest in Ibiza lay also in its vast, still-productive salt flats. The salt was used to cure fish, which was exported (along with a much appreciated local fish sauce) to Carthage, back to Tyre and Sidon and later to neighbouring Mallorca and Menorca. Ibiza also made a tidy profit from its exports of wool and dyes for textiles.

The Romans

The Romans never really infiltrated Ibiza. Even after they defeated the Carthaginian general Hannibal in 202 BC, the Romans' influence was restrained. Only with the fall of

Gods and Goddesses

Ibiza's gods have always been a lusty lot. Originating in the eastern Mediterranean, the deities revered by the Carthaginians were imbued with a sensuality that has remained the island's trademark. Surviving busts of the chief goddess, Tanit, who was worshipped for her fertility, portray her with thick, sensuous lips and luxuriant, flowing hair. She was the consort of Baal Hammon, king of the Carthaginian gods, whom the Romans identified with Saturn. The riotous festivities that took place in his name during what is now the Christmas season are a year-round phenomenon on modern Ibiza.

Many clay figurines have been found in ancient pottery recently unearthed near the Puig des Molins necropolis, below Ibiza Town's Dalt Vila. Most popular of these was the outrageous dwarf god, Bes, often portrayed with goggle eyes, protruding tongue, bow legs, bushy tail and even a crown of feathers. He, too, would probably have enjoyed the island's 21st-century nightlife.

Life and Art in the Carthaginian Colony

Believing that the local clay could repel animals and harmful substances, the Carthaginians considered Ibiza a holy island. From the time of its colonisation by the North African nation, Ibiza grew steadily in importance and for centuries it ranked as one of the major commercial and military centres in the Mediterranean. Decline set in with the defeat of Carthage by the Romans (146 BC), yet Ibiza held fast to the fierce gods and sometimes gruesome customs of the past, preserving the Phoenician traditions of Carthage long into the Roman period.

Archaeologists paint a fascinating picture of life, death and ritual in the Carthaginian colony. More than 20 ancient sites have been explored over the past century and a wealth of objects has come to light. The most important necropolis (burial site) is at Puig des Molins, where there are some 4,000 tombs, though fewer than 300 have actually been uncovered. Here you can see the spacious burial chambers constructed for rich citizens of the capital, who were laid to rest in enormous stone sarcophagi surrounded by the paraphernalia of a happy afterlife: unguent jars, lanterns, terracotta statuettes of deities and ostrich eggs decorated with symbols of life and resurrection. The less affluent made do with a shallow tomb or simple sarcophagus set into the hillside. Cheaper still – if less roomy – was an ordinary vase just large enough to hold the ashes of the departed.

Other important Carthaginian sites include the sanctuaries of Isla Plana, a little peninsula jutting into the Bahía d'Ibiza, and Es Cuieram, a cave near Sant Vicent in the sparsely populated northeastern quadrant of the island. From the earliest period of Carthaginian colonisation, Isla Plana was a holy place. People came here to seek protection, especially from difficulties in childbirth and from childhood illnesses. Es Cuieram was dedicated to the cult of the goddess Tanit, which reached its peak from the 4th to the 2nd centuries BC. The isolation of the cave did not stop believers from depositing gold medallions and hundreds of terracotta figures here. Nearly all the terracotta pieces discovered were blackened by fire. Together with the quantities of bones and ashes uncovered in the cave, this suggests some kind of funerary rite at Es Cuieram.

For all its vitality, the island's Carthaginian culture died out. By the close of the Roman era, Es Cuieram, Isla Plana, Puig des Molins and Ibiza's other sanctuaries and necropolises lay abandoned and forgotten. Then, after the Arab conquests in the 9th and 10th centuries AD, thieves plundered the tombs of Puig des Molins, stripping them of precious gold jewellery. However, the thieves added something of their own to the archaeological record by leaving behind the lamps that illuminated their search.

Sadly, the plunder continued into the 20th century, with unscrupulous archaeologists amassing private collections of Carthaginian art and artefacts in the course of 'official' excavations. There were plenty of clandestine digs, too. One antiques dealer from Mallorca kept a legion of islanders on the lookout for additions to his collection. He later exhibited the finds in Barcelona and pocketed the proceeds. Not long afterwards, Barcelona's archaeological museum acquired every last object for a handsome sum.

Although many key pieces of Carthaginian art have been dispersed or lost, many more are on display in Ibiza's archaeological museums. Gold work, jewellery, the painted spheres of ostrich eggs and exquisitely modelled terracottas all provide rare but valuable insight into the island's past. These ritual and ornamental objects perplex and intrigue. Even in their paucity, they do at least offer a tantalising glimpse of the spirit of Carthage which Rome had been so determined to destroy.

Carthage in 146BC did they manage to make inroads. However – as local historians proudly emphasise – Ibiza was neither conquered nor annexed by Rome but confederated, retaining considerable autonomy. For centuries to come the old Carthaginian traditions were allowed to continue on Ibiza alongside the new Roman way of life.

On the other hand, the empire left a far more decisive imprint on the Iberian Peninsula, where language, culture and government were all heavily influenced by Rome and where, in particular, the Romans' engineering genius was evident in the construction of roads, aqueducts and monuments.

The Romans did exploit Ibiza's natural resources. They exported salt from the southern end of the island and lead from the mines of Sant Carles, and they carried on the

Tunnel to the past: through an old bulwark and into Dalt Vila. These splendid fortifications are several centuries old.

Phoenician technique of extracting a purple dye from shell-fish, which was used for imperial cloaks. In addition, they found a money-spinner in the islanders' exotic aromatic sauce of decomposed fish innards. Called *garum*, it was considered a great delicacy by Romans and Greeks alike. Today it is just a historical footnote; local cooks now use nothing more pungent than garlic.

The Arabs

After prolonged peace and productivity, the year AD 426 launched an era of strife and violence. Ibiza, along with the rest of Spain, was invaded and sacked by the Germanic tribe of Vandals. Centuries of foreign rule followed, with the Vandals succeeded first by the Byzantines and then by Arab forces, which attacked Ibiza in 711.

Rebounding from initial defeats by the Carolingian armies of the Franks, the Arabs had completed their conquest of the Balearic Islands by 903. They alternated sporadic violent forays of piracy on the high seas with equally energetic development of the islands' economy and agriculture. The Arabs' ingenious network of irrigation ditches is still in operation on Ibiza. Most enduring of their legacies is the pure North African design of the houses, justly admired by the great Swiss architect Le Corbusier: simple combinations of dazzling white, round-cornered cubes, thick-walled to keep cool in summer and warm in winter.

Apart from a few ceramics in the museum, the artistic achievements of the Arabs survive best in the island's haunting folk music. Otherwise, the Islamic heritage crops up in a few local place names, some words amalgamated into the Ibicenco language, and – most vivid reminder of all – the dark, brooding eyes of so many islanders. Spanish writers still refer to their North African colonisers as 'Moors', and

Europeans generally use the term 'Moorish' to refer to anything reflecting the pan-Arab culture of the medieval and Renaissance periods.

Christianity Comes to Ibiza

In the 12th century Ibiza was drawn into the ongoing fight between Islamic and Christian forces for control of the Mediterranean world. With the Crusaders' wars raging in Palestine and Syria, a Christian fleet arrived in Ibiza harbour on what was known as the Crusade of Pisa *(see below)* as part of a papal effort to break the Arabs' control on Spanish territory and to punish their brazen pirates.

Although this little local crusade of 1113 did not put an end to the Arab presence, it did herald the end of Islamic power

The Crusade of Pisa

The determination of Pope Paschal II in 1113 to make Ibiza safe for Christianity was not greeted by the islanders with the enthusiasm his Crusaders had been led to expect. The Crusade of Pisa, as it was called, arrived with a fleet of 500 warships to put an end to Islam's hold on the island as well as to the haven Ibiza provided for pirates. Instead of greeting the Christian forces as saviours, the Ibicencos rallied round the Arab viceroy, Abdul Manzor. They repelled one bloody charge after another and turned what the Crusaders had hoped would be a quick-fire invasion into a prolonged siege. In the end, however, people saw that the battle was lost and persuaded their leader to surrender. After dismantling what remained of the battered city walls, the Crusaders gave the islanders their first lesson in Christian piety by raping their women, forcing able-bodied men into service and carrying off all the booty they could grab.

in Ibiza. Just over a century later, the wave of Christian victories over the Arabs on the Spanish mainland, known as the *reconquista* (reconquest) engulfed the island. King Jaume I of Aragón and Catalunya, who had taken Mallorca in 1229, ordered the occupation of the islands under Catalonian forces commanded by Guillermo de Montgri, Bishop of Tarragona. After several bloody skirmishes, the troops launched a final pincer-movement assault on Ibiza's citadel. One flank of soldiers battered its way through the reinforced city walls. The other flank (so the popular story goes) sneaked through

Christian churches sprang up all over the island after the 13th-century reconquest.

a secret passage revealed to the invaders by the brother of the sheik himself. The legend claims the embittered traitor gave the game away because his brother had seduced his wife.

In this violent last act of August 1235, both Christianity and the Catalan language came to Ibiza to stay. On the mainland, the reconquest was practically completed by the earlier Christian victory at Las Navas de Tolosa in northern Andalusia in 1212 and the capture of Córdoba in 1236. However, it was only in 1492 that the Arabs were finally driven out of Granada, their last, brilliant stronghold on the peninsula.

An Era of Pirates

The year 1492 was crucial for Ibiza, and for Spain as a whole, for several reasons. On the mainland it marked the final defeat of the Arabs and – as one of Europe's more momentous forms of 'ethnic cleansing' – the expulsion of Arabs and Jews from the newly united kingdom of the Catholic Monarchs, Ferdinand and Isabella. It was Isabella who expressed the goal of the Spanish Inquisition as achieving *limpieza de sangre* (blood cleansing).

It was also the year Christopher Columbus sailed to the Americas under the Spanish flag. For Ibiza, Spain's enrichment proved to be a catastrophe rather than a boon. The Balearic Islands were not allowed to trade with the new colonies, and the immense wealth of gold and silver brought back by the *conquistadors* diverted the attention of Spain away from the Mediterranean, as they focused on the New World and supremacy over their covetous northern European rivals. Throughout the 16th and 17th centuries, Ibiza sank into a stagnating backwater beset by plague and piracy.

The pirates came in large part from the Barbary Coast of North Africa. The fabled coast – embracing what are now Algeria and Tunisia – took its name from the region's earli-

Piracy on the High Seas

One of the most villainous swashbucklers sailing in Ibizan waters was a Spanish pirate from Gibraltar, Captain Miguel Novelli, alias 'the Pope'. Attacking the island from his cynically-named ship, *Felicity* (meaning happiness), he was confronted one day by Ibicenco Captain Antonio Riquer midway between Ibiza and Formentera. Although Riquer had only eight guns compared to the Pope's dozen cannons, the local vessel won the day.

est inhabitants, the Berbers, but the 16th-century raiders were mainly Turks and Arabs who had been driven out of Spain. Most celebrated of the Turkish pirates was Barbarossa (Redbeard) who, as Khayr Ad-Din, became an admiral in the Ottoman imperial navy.

The Ibicencos fortified the bulwarks of Ibiza Town and built churches throughout the island as massive hilltop bastions against enemy incursions. A chain of sturdy, round, stone watchtowers was constructed all along the island's coast. It is said that even the Ibicenco women's costume of several layers of petticoats was designed to protect them against pirates by simulating pregnancy.

In desperation, the islanders decided to meet fire with fire and formed their own bands of privateers. The local forces were subsequently 'sponsored' by the French and British, who appreciated the islanders' skills in ship building. Suddenly, Barbarossa's pirates and others found their brigantines boarded on the open seas by fierce Ibicencos who commandeered their booty. Victory over the greatly feared 'Pope' *(see panel opposite)* was a much vaunted triumph. Reflecting the morality of a period when piracy was widely regarded as merely an alternative form of commerce, Ibiza's port even raised a monumental obelisk to honour the exploits of its daring, home-grown buccaneers.

Political Turmoil

Ibiza enjoyed a degree of autonomy, first from the kingdom of Aragón, then from united Spain. The island forfeited a small measure of this autonomy in 1715 after supporting the Spanish branch of the Austrian Habsburg dynasty against the victorious Bourbons in the Spanish Wars of Succession. Later, at the end of the 18th century, independent-minded Ibicenco peasants resisted the Spanish government's effort to regroup them into parishes, preferring to remain scattered across the island. And by 1815 the Napoleonic Wars had put an end to pirate raids in the region.

Ibiza thereafter continued to take a back seat as Spain slid into economic decline and political instability, losing the last of its empire in the Americas and the Pacific by 1898. In the first three decades of the 20th century, neither military dictatorship under General Primo de Rivera nor a constitutional monarchy under Alfonso XIII could guarantee domestic tranquillity. The Republican election victory in 1931 drove the king into exile. Strikes, insurrection and brutal military repression spread through the peninsula as the new republic was torn apart by bitter ideological divisions.

In February 1936 the left-wing Popular Front came to power, facing fierce right-wing opposition from the fascist Falangist Party, supported by the church, the army, monar-

Relic from the past. A mill wheel recalls more sedate times in the now buzzing resort of Sant Antoni.

chists and big business. Five months later, a military revolt led by General Francisco Franco plunged the country into a three-year civil war that cost around one million lives.

Like neighbouring Mallorca, Ibiza yielded to its Nationalist garrison at the outbreak of war in July 1936. Among the Balearic Islands, only Menorca resisted the first military rebellion. Then Republican forces chose Ibiza as the bridgehead for a counter-attack. On 9 August a joint Catalan-Valencian force arrived in Ibiza's harbour with four transport ships escorted by a battleship, two destroyers, a submarine and six aircraft. Encouraged by this, Ibicenco workers seized the 50-strong pro-Franco garrison. A subsequent assault on Mallorca failed, but Ibiza (and Formentera) reverted to Republican control.

Modern Times

Franco's Spain stayed neutral throughout World War II but could not repair its own shattered economy. Even after 1945, reconstruction remained painfully slow, helped somewhat when the country was once more recognised by the Western democracies. For Ibiza the breakthrough came with the introduction in the 1960s of wide-bodied jets and a significant surge in sun-seeking tourism. Following the expansion of Es Codolar airport, the island entered the big league of international holiday resorts.

After the death of Franco in 1975, his chosen successor, King Juan Carlos I, restored democracy to Spain, and moderates and democratic socialists emerged as the largest parties in the first free elections in 1977. Following years of repression, new freedoms were granted to Spanish regions, and their languages and cultures enjoyed a long-sought renaissance. The Balearic Islands were granted a degree of autonomy in

Old Ibiza offers a fascinating glimpse of the past.

1978 and five years later became the Comunidad Autónoma de las Islas Baleares. Free speech and free elections were not the only innovations: a new liberalism prevailed; gambling was legalised and nude bathing was sanctioned. Change swept through Ibiza dramatically, rapidly and irrevocably.

The islands' fortunes improved in 1986 when Spain joined the European Community (now European Union). In spite of high unemployment, the country's economic growth rate was among the highest in Europe during the last quarter of the 20th century. By 1996 the wounds of Francoism were healed sufficiently for a centre-right prime minister, José María Aznar, to defeat socialist Felipe González (who led the country for 13 years) without anyone fearing for democracy. Aznar served two terms, then chose his deputy, Mariano Rajoy, to lead the Popular Party into the general elections scheduled for March 2004.

It was also in 1996 that the Balearic Island government initiated measures to protect the environment and encourage eco-friendly tourism throughout the islands. In Ibiza, where the capital's Dalt Villa was declared a UNESCO World Heritage Site in 1999, efforts are now being made to ensure that, while the party spirit is allowed to flourish, the island's environment and its reputation are protected.

Historical Landmarks

600 BC Earliest inhabitants build megalithic monuments.

654 BC Carthaginians colonise Ibiza.

218–201 BC Ibiza's ammunition used in Carthage's war against Rome.

123 BC Ibiza added to Roman confederation.

AD426 Ibiza raided and sacked by Vandals.

903 Arab conquest of Balearic Islands complete.

1235 Christian rulers bring reconquest to Ibiza.

1469 Marriage of Ferdinand II to Isabella unites Spain; Balearics become key Spanish posts in Mediterranean.

1492 Arabs and Jews expelled from Spain; Christopher Columbus sails to the Americas.

1500 Spain's transatlantic preoccupations send Balearics into decline; Barbary Coast piracy begins.

1799–1815 Napoleonic Wars end pirate raids.

1936 Left-wing Republican government opposed by General Franco and fascist Falangist Party.

1936–39 Civil War: Ibiza captured by Republican forces.

1960s Ibiza inundated by mass tourism with introdution of wide-bodied jets and expansion of the airport.

1975 Death of Franco, constitutional monarchy restored.

1978 Statute of Autonomy; five years later the Balearic Islands become a semi-autonomous province, and their language, a version of Catalan, is given official status.

1986 Spain joins European Community, now European Union.

1996 José María Aznar replaces socialist Felipe Gonzalez as Spanish prime minister. Contre-right Partido Popular in government until the present date.

1999 Ibiza's Dalt Vila declared a UNESCO World Heritage Site.

2002 The euro becomes the official currency of Spain.

2004 Spanish general election scheduled for March.

WHERE TO GO

Some visitors to these islands don't want to go far – they simply stay put and enjoy the sun and sea, wandering from hotel to beach and back again. Others want to explore the island of Ibiza, starting with its three main urban centres: Eivissa (Ibiza Town), Sant Antoni and Santa Eulària. Some head for the interior to explore the classically Mediterranean landscape, dotted with white Ibicenco farmhouses, and find time to drive around the magical, rugged coastline.

An excursion to Formentera reveals a different landscape and scene: a desert island that is more relaxed, more rural and thus more traditional. The beaches are less crowded and the overall atmosphere is laid back and lazy. Nevertheless, Formentera has resorts, hotels, restaurants and nightclubs to satisfy those needing a few reminders of the high life.

IBIZA

Morning, noon and night there is a feast for the senses everywhere you look on Ibiza – and you are often tempted to look everywhere at once. At breakfast time near the harbour in any of the major resorts you can drink coffee in one of the port-side cafés, and watch the activity as the fishing boats come in or the elegant yachts prepare to go out. Mid-morning in Eivissa you might want to wander round the boutiques of the Sa Penya quarter, or walk up through the old Dalt Vila (Upper Town) citadel to explore the fascinating Phoenician past in the museum or the rich Spanish Catholic culture in the cathedral.

After strolling up to the hilltop church in Santa Eulària for a view over the bay, you might develop an appetite, which you can satisfy at a variety of excellent restaurants. Then spend a lazy or an active afternoon (depending on your inclination) in the sun, sea and sand at any one of 56 beaches stretching around the island *(see page 41).*

Nature lovers will want to explore the many beautiful trails in the interior to take in the fragrances and colours of the wildflowers *(see page 58).* On the way, enjoy a little bird-watching along the cliffs or on the salt flats of Ses Salines *(see page 48).* Among your other options is a boat cruise to explore the coastline and discover otherwise inaccessible secluded coves for swimming and diving. Or you can make a full day's outing to the island of Formentera.

That leaves the evening for a quiet meal or a boisterous party – or maybe both – in one of the many hot spots in and around Sant Antoni and other major resorts.

The island is divided administratively into five communes (districts): Eivissa (Ibiza Town), Sant Antoni, Santa Eulària, Sant Josep and Sant Joan, each named after its principal urban centre. We visit each of the communes as we explore the towns, resorts, villages, hills and coastline of Ibiza.

Ibiza's landscape is bright with blossom at most seasons of the year.

Eivissa (Ibiza Town)

The major focus of activity on the island is, naturally enough, its capital, **Eivissa (Ibiza Town)**, which is divided into four areas. Towering over it all is the old walled city, Dalt Vila (Upper Town). Between the ramparts and the port, La Marina, is the main harbour district, packed with shops, bars, cafés and restaurants. More modest is Sa Penya, a former fishing neighbourhood extending east along the harbour's promontory. The modern district of Eixample (Ensanche in Castilian) stretches west and north from the town's main boulevard, Passeig Vara de Rey.

Most visitors who come alone or with a group for a sightseeing day in Eivissa arrive by bus from one of the outlying resorts. The buses stop on Avinguda Isidoro Macabich, either at the station or opposite the building housing the offices of the island government.

Nothing sleepy about this port – Eivissa's harbour is a constant flurry of arrivals and departures.

Follow Isidoro Macabich east to the major intersection at Avinguda Ignacio Wallis. Turn right and a few hundred metres/yards later you'll come to **Passeig Vara de Rey**, the town's attractive, tree-lined esplanade, which some locals still call by its old name, S'Alamera (The Boulevard). As in most Spanish towns, this is where the young and old alike gather in the early evening for the time-honoured promenade. It owes its present name to one of the island's great heroes, General Joaquín Vara de Rey, commemorated here by a grand, rousing statue surrounded on its pedestal by bronze wreaths and allegorical figures. It was erected six years after the general died defending the colony of Cuba in the Spanish–American War of 1898.

A newsagent here sells a wide selection of European publications. Pick up your favourite paper and take it to one of several outdoor cafés where a *café con leche* can last through a whole morning of basking in the sun, postcard writing, map reading, or watching the crowds. The cafés situated nearest to the port attract the chic and sophisticated, among others, who sit at tables covered with yellow tablecloths and are served by waiters dressed – with exaggerated formality by local standards – in smart bow ties and white jackets. This is also where the town tycoons transact business in the civilised Spanish way, over sherry or brandy.

La Marina and Sa Penya

Now it's time for a tour of the town. The most logical place to start is down at the harbour, around the corner from Vara de Rey. An imposing pier in the centre of the dock area serves the liners from Palma, Barcelona, Valencia and other scheduled ferry points. The passenger terminal is a modern building with a restaurant on top. From there, or from the quayside, there is plenty of activity to see as the gleaming

Island Highlights

Ibiza

Eivissa/Ibiza Town: the harbour, La Marina and the atmospheric old-world streets of Sa Penya.

Dalt Vila: the old walled town, with sturdy defences, the cathedral and museums; a UNESCO World Heritage Site.

Museu Monogràfic del Puig des Molins: this is the one museum that should not be missed, as it gives the best view of Ibiza's Phoenician beginnings.

Sant Antoni: once a fishing village, now a resort with a yacht-filled bay, fishing and ferry boats and good beaches.

Sa Conillera: the uninhabited island where Hannibal is said to have been born; good for escaping the crowds and for walks among wildflowers and lizards.

Santa Eulària: former market centre and the first town to attract foreign visitors, it has a fine selection of restaurants.

Sa Talaia: also known as Atalaya, at 475m (1,560ft) the highest point on the island; a challenging drive and/or hike, with magnificent views.

Es Cuieram: a secluded cave that was used as a Carthaginian burial ground; treasures uncovered here are now on view in the archaeological museum in Dalt Vila.

Ses Salines: extensive salt flats that can be found on both Ibiza and Formentera.

Formentera

Far de sa Mola: 19th-century lighthouse featured in Jules Verne's *Journey Round the Solar System*, occupying a splendid position with wonderful views of Formentera.

Ca Na Costa: prehistoric stone circle dating from about 1600BC, still being excavated but open for viewing.

white ships load and unload their cargo and passengers. In front of the terminal, a roundabout now surrounds the **Monument al Corsaris**, perhaps the world's only monument in praise of privateers.

The district of **La Marina**, extending inland from the monument to the old city walls, combines the traditional image of a Mediterranean port with all the modern amenities of a bustling tourist area. One white church is dedicated to the quarter's patron saint, known variously as Sant Elm or Sant Salvador. Beyond the church in the direction of the old walled city is the **Mercat de ses Verdures** (fruit and vegetable market). In the narrow streets, classical Ibicenco houses – white cubic forms, many leaning at an angle, their black wrought-iron balconies decked out with a few flowers – have been transformed into fashion boutiques and souvenir shops, with goods cascading onto the pavements. More colour is added by visitors' gaudy holiday clothes, while the whole scene is observed from bars and cafés by sleepy night owls shading their eyes against the bright sun.

In the neighbourhood named after the harbour promontory, **Sa Penya** (The Rock), the streets are even narrower and noticeably poorer. Tourist cafés and restaurants are largely confined to the waterfront. At night this district is a popular entertainment area. By day, as the streets climb toward Dalt Vila, a few fishermen can still be seen making their way home, passing black-clad women laden with shopping. Passers-by should watch out for the drips from laundry drying on balconies above and for scampering children or loping dogs and cats underfoot. Wafting out of the windows are the aromas of coffee, spices, fish and baking bread. The octagonal **Mercat de Peix** (fish market) is close to the ramparts of the old city.

Dalt Vila

Opposite the fruit and vegetable market is the main entrance to the old walled citadel, **Dalt Vila** (there are two other ancient gateways through the walls). A ceremonial ramp leads across what used to be a moat into an impressive gateway, the **Portal de ses Taules**. Over the arch is a Latin inscription dating the wall to 1585, during the reign of Felipe II of Spain. Standing on either side are gracefully robed, headless, white marble statues. They were unearthed on the spot during a 16th-century construction project. According to the barely decipherable Latin inscriptions, one of the statues honours a Roman senator; the other is a tribute from an aristocratic Roman family to Juno, the Roman goddess.

Historians believe the Carthaginians initially constructed a wall here – with foundations shared by the current city walls – although none of it remains. The Arabs built a second wall, of which towers and remnants are evident today. Ibiza's seven bulwark defences are almost entirely intact. The present bulwarks date back to 1554, when Emperor Carlos V ordered reconstruction of the wall, which had a thickness of 3.5m (11.5ft). The fortifications, which are among the best preserved in Europe, were declared a UNESCO World Heritage Site in 1999. They still completely encircle the old citadel and remain an admirable testimony to the military technology of the Renaissance.

The tunnel through the great wall at Portal de Ses Taules leads to a classic quadrangle planned for royal parades, the **Plaça de la Vila**. Today, the pomp under the porticos has been replaced by artisans peddling their jewellery and leatherwork, often original and inexpensive. The square, which also houses the **Museu d'Art Contemporani**, leads into the first of several wide, open plazas linked by a maze of narrow alleys climbing the citadel hill.

A map isn't really necessary in Dalt Vila, an old town of steep cobbled streets, curious dead ends, and unexpected vistas. The most important directions are simply up and down: 'up' leads eventually to the hilltop cathedral and fortress, and 'down' inevitably leads to one of three gates through the wall to the new town. The variations are almost infinite and this is one time when wrong turns can actually be recommended. Every zigzag is likely to bring another delight – a sweep of bougainvillaea, a baroque doorway, a fashionable restaurant, or a new perspective on the sea and city below.

The main entrance to Dalt Vila, Portal de ses Taules.

When you reach an impressive plaza with a 16th-century church and whitewashed town hall, you might feel you've come to the top of the town. But you haven't. Catch your breath here and admire the view down the cliffside from the edge of the city wall before continuing to ascend the narrow streets.

At last you reach the uppermost cobbled square, the Plaça Catedral. The **Catedral de Santa Maria de las Neus** (Our Lady of the Snows), on the right, was built in the 14th century on the site of a Roman temple and an Islamic mosque, and renovated in the 16th and 18th centuries. The resulting architectural eccentricities on the exterior are matched in interest by the medieval works of art inside. More works can be seen in the adjacent museum. If you wonder why, in this sunny climate, the church is dedicated to Our Lady of the Snows, it is because the Catalan rulers chose the patron saint whose feast day, 5 August, came closest to the date of their victory over the Arabs, three days later.

Across the square is the **Museu Arqueològic de Dalt Vila** (Archaeological Museum), which houses Roman, Islamic and Carthaginian antiquities. Together with the Museu Monogràfic *(see below)*, this constitutes what is believed to be the world's greatest treasury of Carthaginian artefacts. All the relics on display were discovered on the island; they range from statues and urns and fertility figures to priceless jewellery and coins. The museum, which occupies part of what was once the town's university, is compact enough to be covered in about an hour.

> When visiting churches, you should not wear shorts, tank tops, or backless dresses.

Puig des Molins

Making your way over to Portal Nou, another gateway through the great wall, you will find yourself in the modern part of town amid offices, luxury apartments and shops. Four streets away is the **Museu Monogràfic del Puig des Molins**, a modern, spacious museum. It is built on the edge of an attractive hill, which is covered with gnarled olive trees and wildflowers and is known as **Puig des Molins** (Hill of the Windmills), although the windmills are long gone. Here, the Carthaginians, and later the Romans, buried their dead with respectful ritual. The artefacts displayed in the museum were all unearthed on the spot. Outstanding among them is a terracotta bust of the Carthaginian goddess *(see page 35 for opening times of both museums).*

Museums and Galleries

Note: All the listed museums are in Eivissa.

Museu Arqueològic de Dalt Vila (Plaça Catedral). Exhibits from all over the island, especially Carthaginian terracottas and fertility figures from sanctuaries and necropolises, plus a selection of Roman and Arabic artefacts. Open Apr–Sept: Tues–Sat 10am–2pm and 5–8pm, Sun 10am–2pm; Oct–Mar:Tues–Sat 10am–1pm and 4–6pm, Sun 10am–2pm.

Museu Monogràfic del Puig des Molins (Via Romana). On display are articles discovered in the Carthaginian necropolis nearby, including scarabs, unguent jars, jewellery, mirrors and razors. Superb collection of terracottas. Be sure to take a look at the powerful series of goddesses, imperial in their elaborate necklaces, gold nose-rings and earrings. Visit the necropolis itself, where several burial chambers are open to view. Open Apr–Sept: daily 5–8pm; Oct–Mar: 4–7pm.

Museu del Catedral (adjacent to Ibiza's cathedral, at the summit of the old town). Contains municipal and church memorabilia. One particularly interesting item is a monstrance (receptacle for the host) from Mallorca, a prized example of medieval silverware dating from the late-15th century. Open Apr–Sept: daily 10am–1pm; Oct–Apr: Tues and Fri 10am–1pm.

Museu d'Arte Contemporani (Baluarte de Sant Joan, Ronda Narcis Puget, just inside the old town). Modern art, one-man shows, and group exhibitions in a venerable setting. Open Apr–Sept: Tues–Fri 10am–2pm and 4–6pm; Sat–Sun10am–1.30pm.

Art galleries. There are galleries in Eivissa and on the road to Sant Josep and Sant Miquel, as well as in Sant Antoni and Santa Eulària. Special shows are advertised. The island attracts artists of all styles and levels of expertise, and the sheer volume of their output is prodigious. Ibiza's artists also display their works in many tourist hotels and expatriate bars.

Outside and around the corner of the building you'll find a cave-like entrance to the necropolis, the funerary site itself, where several burial chambers have been cleared and illuminated. There are some 4,000 vaults in all. If you've seen the museum's works of art – which were buried next to the bodies – the necropolis shouldn't seem too gloomy. If you feel a little claustrophobic, then wander to the far side of the hill for a view of the sea and, on a clear day, Formentera. Nearby is the beach of **Figueretes**, which means 'little fig trees', and is a popular place for swimming.

Sant Antoni

From Ibiza Town, a short drive to the west coast of the island brings you to **Sant Antoni.** Until the late 1960s Sant Antoni was a pretty, low-key little fishing port, but it has been transformed into a large-scale, exuberant tourist resort that keeps expanding its boundaries ever farther around and beyond the town's magnificent bay. Under the Romans, the grand sweep of the harbour earned it the name Portus Magnus, which survives today in the town's full name, Sant Antoni de Portmany.

Many people may regret the changes to the town, and the fact that the few remaining fishing boats have to make their way around sleek yachts and powerful motor launches, passing glass-bottomed boats, big ferries, and even bigger freighters. The municipal authorities and local entrepreneurs, on the other hand, are delighted by the prosperity brought by mass tourism. Gleaming white, high-rise hotels have sprung up, catering to apparently tireless guests who satisfy their appetite for life in some of the island's most boisterous bars and discos.

With Sant Antoni's local population close to 15,000, the ongoing expansion has its pros and cons. The newer hotels have been built on out-of-town beaches, providing swimming and sunbathing on the doorstep but requiring trransport to shopping and nightlife. Conversely, those staying in town sometimes have to travel to find a desirable beach. To compensate, buses seem to go everywhere and there are ferry connections as well. Part of the Sant Antoni adventure is planning each day's outing with the help of local maps and bus timetables. The west coast of Ibiza has a terrific choice of first-rate beaches – all an easy day-trip from Sant Antoni – suitable for children, windsurfers and scuba divers.

The town itself has managed to preserve a few of its old stucco houses among the brash new buildings. The sturdy, white 14th-century church of **Sant Antoni** has an elevated position overlooking the bay. It replaced an Islamic mosque and once served as a fortress, with a watchtower to warn against assaults by pirates and other invaders. Its formidable appearance is softened by an attractive patio surrounded by graceful arches.

Along the waterfront, the centre of activity is the **Passeig Marítim** (Maritime Promenade), reclaimed from the sea and now lined with palms, beneath which are benches, a fountain and a proliferation of outdoor cafés and restaurants.

Small ferryboats (mostly converted fishing vessels)

In the past, Sant Antoni has also served as a fortress.

operate to beaches near and far; generally speaking, the beaches farther away from town are better. All those served by public transport have snack bars, beach chairs, sun loungers and parasols for hire, as well as other amenities. Lifeguards, however, are rare on Ibiza, with practically none on duty on a regular, all-day basis.

The municipal bus station is right next to the seafront promenade. Buses to the beaches are cheaper and faster than ferries, if less adventurous, but the bus service is restricted to beaches close to the town. The island's rugged topography and municipal politics have so far prevented a road going all the way round the coast, so many of the best beaches can be reached only on bumpy, dusty trails more suitable for mules than buses.

You can take a trip on the little road train, the Sant Antoni Express, which stops near the famous Columbus Egg sculpture at the south end of town.

Dominating the mouth of Sant Antoni Bay is the gaunt silhouette of the island of **Sa Conillera**, which means 'rabbit warren' or 'burrow'. According to legend, this uninhabited island was the birthplace of the Carthaginian warrior, Hannibal. Its other claim to fame is an automatic lighthouse with a signal visible at distances of up to 48km (30 miles). From Sant Antoni, Sa Conillera appears to be almost hopelessly inhospitable, but a tiny, hidden harbour makes it possible for boats to moor there. The island is well covered with tenacious pines, a delightful variety of wildflowers and crowds of friendly lizards. The swimming is unsuitable for children, however, and it is a good idea to wear plastic sandals to protect against the spiny quills of sea urchins.

An excursion 2km (1 mile) north from Sant Antoni leads to the early Christian subterranean chapel of **Santa Inés** (open Mon 9am–noon and Sat 7–9pm), built complete with nave and chancel inside a natural cave. Excavations here in 1907 uncovered artefacts from Carthaginian, Roman and Arab eras.

Also north of the town is another natural cave, converted into an aquarium, the Aquario Cap Blanc (open daily 10.30am–sunset). You can reach it via a little path beside the sea, starting outside the Hotel Tanit.

Santa Eulària

On the south coast – east of Eivissa – is the island's second-largest town, **Santa Eulària** (population 19,500).

The elaborate baroque altar in Santa Eulària's fine church.

It has grown into a prosperous resort with a pleasant, light-hearted atmosphere that seems less frenetic than that of its rival, Sant Antoni. Foreign artists and writers made their home here long before commercial tourism arrived and can justly claim credit for the town's enduring reputation for good restaurants and bars.

The only river on Ibiza, with its source barely 12km (7 miles) to the north, near Santa Gertrudis, gives the town its formal name: Santa Eulària del Riu. The river was once used by the Arabs for irrigation, establishing the town's role as an agricultural centre. Ever-increasing water consumption has reduced the river to little more than a trickle today, but Santa Eulària is still surrounded by fruit and vegetable gardens, green pine forests and extensive farmlands to the north. Its administrative district comprises the towns of Santa Gertrudis, Sant Carles and Jesús and stretches along the island's southeast coast from Cap Martinet, near Talamanca, almost all the way north to Cala Sant Vicent.

Santa Eulària is divided into two distinct areas: the old, inland community nestled around the church on **Puig de Missa** hill, and the modern town that has extended in more peaceful times down to the port. Atop Puig de Missa, the dazzling white **Església de Santa Eulària** is worth a visit both for historic interest and the magnificent view over the bay. The core of the fortress church was built in 1568 by Italian architect Giovanni Battista Calvi, who followed up the ramparts for Eivissa with a similarly sturdy defensive tower here. Chapels on either side of the presbytery were added in the 17th century to complete the cruciform floor plan. There is a delightful flower garden in the cemetery. The little hill also offers a view of the river and its two bridges, one modern and one old and cobbled, possibly Roman in origin.

One of the island's characteristic cubic white houses has been transformed into a small folkloric museum, the **Museu Etnològic** (open Tues–Sat 11am–1pm, 5–8pm, Sun–Mon 5–8pm), displaying domestic and agricultural tools, toys and traditional costumes.

In the modern district of **Sa Vila Nova**, the arcaded town hall (Ajuntament) looks out across a plaza down a broad esplanade to the seafront. A monument on the plaza commemorates a shipwreck of 1913. Having shed the name Passeig Generalissimo Franco, the tree-lined esplanade is now popularly known as La Rambla, in architectural homage to Barcelona's celebrated thoroughfare. On the seafront promenade, Passeig Marítim, people stroll past the cafés and shops along the splendid sweep of Santa Eulària bay from the yachting harbour west to the mouth of the river.

Island Beaches

Ibiza

Cala Comte: panoramic sandy and rocky beach; suitable for both snorkellers and children.

Cala Llonga: a shallow bay surrounded by pine groves; fine white sand, good for young children; restaurants, sunbeds, pedalos, windsurfing.

Cala Tárida: white sand and flat rocks, an activity-oriented beach with plenty of water sports; restaurant and beach bar.

Cala Vedella: popular but often busy family beach, with fine white sand flanked by rocks; lots of amenities, including bars, pedalos, windsurfing.

Es Canar: popular sandy beach and cove with fine sands and a backdrop of pine woods; a favourite for water sports enthusiasts but safe for children, too.

Platja Cavallet: the island's official nudist beach (but good for birdwatching, too), with fine white sand plus rocks at its southern end; complete with amenities but little shade.

Platja d'en Bossa: known as the island's longest beach (2.5km/1.5 miles), close to Eivissa and very busy; popular especially for its lively beach bar; pedalos and schools for diving and motor boating.

Formentera

Cala Saona: attractive sandy beach, the most popular on Formentera and often busy.

Platja de Migjorn: stretching around a wide bay, a pebbly beach that is Formentera's longest (8km/5 miles).

Platja es Pujols: for many, the best beach on the island, despite the nearby modern construction; good sands, shallow water and lots of amenities.

The Island's Interior

The main road linking Eivissa with Sant Antoni passes through the farming village of Sant Rafel. The 18th-century church is notable for its façade and belfry, with baroque curves that are a rarity on Ibiza. The little plaza in front offers a fine view down over groves of orange, almond and fig trees to the distant sky-line of Eivissa. However, Sant Rafel's most celebrated spot is the island's most notorious disco, the extravagant Privilege (just southeast of town), so beware of the late-night traffic on this already busy highway. Of course, if you can't beat 'em, join 'em. In the more tranquil daylight hours, visit the local pottery workshops.

A smaller road farther to the west also links Sant Antoni to Eivissa. From it, a signposted turn-off just west of Sant Josep takes you along roads – first paved, then bumpy dirt tracks – to the island's highest point, **Sa Talaia**, 475m (1,560ft) above sea level. Its name, meaning 'The Watchtower', is justified by the grand view over the southern half of the island and, on a clear day, west to the Spanish mainland, and by the remains of an old fortress at the top.

The village of **Sant Josep** is capital of the island's largest commune, covering all of southern Ibiza from the bay of Sant Antoni east to Playa d'en Bossa. In an enchanting setting of juniper, fig, carob and pine trees, its immaculate, white, cuboid houses are embellished with well-tended flower gardens.

> You can walk up to Sa Talaia if you have the stamina – it takes about 2½ hours, starting outside the church.

Sant Josep proudly maintains local customs and is well known for its craftwork. Several shops sell local embroidery and galleries display the work of island artists. The town regularly shows its attachment to local traditions with colourful displays of dancing in the forecourt of the Església de Sant Josep. The music strikingly combines the rhythms of Arabic music with songs of the Christian era. The bell-towered church, like that of Sant Antoni, was damaged by fire at the outbreak of the Spanish Civil War. The baroque altarpiece was completely destroyed but has been replaced by a faithful replica. The handsome, original wooden rosary pulpit, created in 1763 by José Sànchez Ocaña, remains intact.

Rustic earthenware pottery in Sant Josep, a town renowned for its crafts.

Just south of the Sant Josep–Eivissa road, the illuminated stalactites and stalagmites of the 25-m (82-ft) deep **Cova Santa** (Holy Cave; open Mon–Sat 9.30am–1.30pm) make it a popular attraction. Theories vary about the derivation of the name but it is known to have been used as a sanctuary for people fleeing pirate attacks during the 16th to 18th centuries.

A short drive northeast from Ibiza Town, the village of **Jesús** has, in its solid, 15th-century **Església de Nostra Mare de Deu**, one of the island's most important artistic treasures. Incorporating late Gothic and Italian Renaissance influences, the triptych altar screen (c. 1498) is attributed to the Valencian workshop of Rodrigo de Osona. The church is usually closed but you can ask for the key in the Bar Lloc nearby; or enquire at the Eivissa tourist office (see page 121) about group visits.

A few miles southwest of Eivissa, on the way to the airport, is the pretty little village of **Sant Jordi**. Here you will see one of the most remarkable of all the island's many churches that have had to serve as both house of worship and fortress to defend the community. This church has the imposing battle-

Spirits and Whitewash

Some country folk in the island's interior still practise elements of pre-Christian pagan beliefs and rituals. In many Ibicenco hamlets, old women credited with supernatural powers treat ailing people and animals. These spiritual healers use incantations and herbal medicines.

According to tradition, certain bottles contain little devils or imps *(diablillos)*. If a housewife opens the bottle without following the proper procedure, she is plagued by all manner of minor domestic problems. That, at least, is what she can claim if everything goes wrong.

Every springtime the hardy women of Ibiza set out with almost religious enthusiasm to whitewash their houses. Some anthropologists believe that this custom may be derived from some remote Phoenician ritual. Local poet Fajarnes Cardona referred to it as 'that whiteness, an exorcism of all that's sordid'.

Architects point out that each house represents a conjunction of modular one-room units, infinitely expandable to suit conditions. Instead of the traditional Spanish patio, Ibiza has opted for open verandas with stately arches. Triangular-topped chimneys, outside staircases and the rounded cubic shapes (probably inherited centuries ago from North African settlers, Phoenicians or Arabs) have inspired modern architects all over the world.

ments and solid rectangular form of a castle keep; there is only a little belfry with a cross on top to indicate that it is, in fact, a church. The largely 16th-century edifice replaced a smaller medieval church. With the danger of pirate attacks receding, more graceful arched and domed side chapels were added in the 18th century.

In the northwest of the island, in Sant Miquel de Balansat, the 14th-century **Església de Sant Miquel**, believed to be the oldest church on the island, affords a hilltop view of the distant sea. Inside, the chapel walls and vaults are decorated with unusual, mostly black and white, frescoes. The churchyard has an interesting collection of artefacts, including a wine press and grain mill. Early on Thursday evening in the square outside, traditionally-dressed dancers perform to the music of an authentic local band.

Other inland villages worth exploring in the relatively uncrowded northern half of the island are **Santa Agnés de Corona**, high on a plateau; **Sant Mateu**, beautifully set among almond, fig and olive trees; **Sant Joan de Labritja**, with an enchanting little church and cemetery surrounded by fragrant pines; and the lively **Sant Carles de Peralta**, set amid fertile farmland and famous for Las Dalias hippie market held just outside the village on Saturdays. Finally, **Santa Gertrudis de Fruitera**, right in the centre of the island, is well known for bars selling excellent tapas and *bocadillos* (sandwiches) and for several art galleries, displaying the work of local and expatriate artists.

Around the Coast

The easiest way to explore Ibiza's 170km (105 miles) of coastline is obviously by boat, but drivers can reach many of the fine beaches and enjoy much of the glorious coastline with careful planning and map reading. Be aware however that there is no continuous coastal road; you often have to go some distance inland if you want to travel from one beach to another.

Starting at the top of the compass and working clockwise round the island, the northernmost tourist centre is **Portinatx** (pronounced 'port-ee-*natch*'). To get there from the fertile farmland of the centre, you drive over substantial hills, beside cliffs, and finally down to a surprisingly placid sea. The natural beauty of the area – sandy beaches, unusual rock formations and picturesque groves of juniper and pines – has brought development that is not quite so attractive.

Local historians point out that during Spanish naval manoeuvres just off Ibiza in 1929, Alfonso XIII came ashore here. Immediately, the name of the place was officially changed to Portinatx del Rey. Perhaps, from an international point of view, a more momentous event was the shooting of part of the film *South Pacific* on Portinatx beach.

A bit farther down the east coast, the splendid cove of **Cala de Sant Vicenç** is an increasingly successful resort centre.

A haven fit for a king – Portinatx nestles between cliffs and is marked by unusual rock formations.

While exceptionally hilly and circuitous, the road is good enough to handle a stream of tourist buses, and the beach itself is likely to be crowded. Up in the hills behind Cala de Sant Vicenç, after a rough hike over sometimes difficult terrain, you can visit a cave called **Es Cuieram** (4th century BC). Many archaeological treasures, including statues of fertility goddesses, have been unearthed here in the grounds of an ancient temple dedicated to the Carthaginian goddess, Tanit. Most of the artefacts can be seen in the archaeological museums in Dalt Vila and Puig des Molins. The cave itself is a good place to seek shelter from the midday sun.

Much of the coastline south of Sant Vicenç is good, sandy beach, very popular with visitors from Sant Carles – tourists and local people alike. Areas served by roads have been built up and tend to be crowded in high summer. You have to wander farther afield, or come by boat, to find more seclusion.

Almost due east of Sant Carles is the offshore isle of **Tagomago**, now linked to the Ibizan mainland by regular excursion boats. Although the beach here is too narrow for sunbathing, the swimming is superb. It's worth the effort to ramble up to the lighthouse at the top of the hill, past various abandoned farms amid fields of wildflowers, for the sweeping sea vistas you will encounter along the way.

Es Canar has become a major tourist centre that now sprawls along several beaches. There is plenty of nightlife, but it is a family-oriented resort, with safe, shallow waters. There's another popular weekly hippie market in nearby **Punta Arabí** (May–Oct: Wed 10am–7pm), to which special bus services and excursions run from Santa Eulària. It is also a pickpocket's paradise, so watch your belongings carefully.

Hikers may want to try the coastal path from Es Canar southwest to Santa Eulària and beyond. It winds its way past piney coves, mysterious cliffs and quiet beaches. For some this might sound like hard work, but don't despair, as beach-bar refreshment is never far away.

To the south of Santa Eulària, **Cala Llonga** is just what its name describes: a long cove that, from several vantage points,

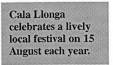

Cala Llonga celebrates a lively local festival on 15 August each year.

looks like a Norwegian fjord. There has been a lot of development here over the years. Hotels and apartment buildings push back into the hills, and their guests join local people and day-trippers from Santa Eulària on a wide, sandy beach that is sheltered and safe for children.

An impressive rocky coastline with a backdrop of verdant hills continues southwards to **Talamanca**, a heavily developed beach with a fine view of Eivissa. On the other side of the capital is the beach and hotel complex of **Ses Figueretes**, and then the 3-km (2-mile) long beach and palm-lined seafront of **Platja d'en Bossa**. This is a package-holiday destination, busy throughout the summer, but it has good facilities, and there's a big water park, **Aguamar**, that is very popular with children *(see page 77)*.

Near the salt flats at the southern tip of the island are some hard-to-reach, mostly unspoiled beaches. Among them is **Platja des Cavallet**, which is officially reserved for nude bathing. The sprawling salt flats of **Ses Salines**, nearly 400 hectares (990 acres) of land lying at or just below sea level, have a fascination of their own. They resemble a desert outpost in an otherwise green and hospitable land, and the white mountains of salt and shimmering patterns on the heavy water remind some people of the Dead Sea. Providing the mainstay of the economy for this area, some 54,400 metric tons (60,000 tons) of salt a year are harvested here. Other nearby attractions include the port called **La Canal**, from which the salt is exported.

Sandy and rocky beaches continue north and west from the salt flats, but they become less and less accessible. The scenery is more spectacular where the hamlet of **Es Cubells** (reached by road from Sant Josep) occupies a land's-end

Wildlife Watch

Ibiza is home to a rare, indigenous dog. The Ibicenco hound is as skinny – and as fast – as a greyhound but has a coat that is typically red with white markings. It has a long snout, big, alert ears and eyes as mysterious as a Siamese cat's. This hungry-looking creature (*podenco* to the islanders) has a history dating back thousands of years, perhaps to the dog portrayed on the walls of ancient Egyptian temples. It is said to be less intelligent than most common mongrels but was introduced to the United States in the 1950s and exhibited at dog shows in the 'miscellaneous class'.

Strictly nocturnal, the little spotted or striped genet can be seen – very rarely – hunting its even smaller prey up in the mountain woods. In fact, there are no truly dangerous animals or poisonous insects or plants on Ibiza. The only reptiles are harmless lizards, of which there are two dozen varieties, usually found sunning themselves on rocks or foraging among pine cones. One species of lizard might be found in your hotel, possibly clinging to the ceiling. Don't disturb them – they are useful allies, as they they catch mosquitoes.

Birdwatchers will enjoy classifying a variety of species that use the Balearics as a stopover during migration. The salt flats of Ibiza and Formentera are good places to spot the wood-sandpiper (distinguished by its greenish-yellow legs).You can also find the raucous bittern, tufted heron, black-winged stilt, the rare Audouin seagull, Eleonora's falcon, and bald buzzard. On rocky coastlines you might catch a rare glimpse of the black and white Manx shearwater (*Puffinus puffinus*, also known to Mediterranean people as the 'Englishman's puffin').

position overlooking rocks and the blue sea. A theological seminary is perched idyllically above the rocky crest.

A bit further up the island's southwest coast, reached via a well-surfaced road, is **Cala d'Hort**, a small, isolated cove with clear waters. Attractive enough in its own right, this peaceful little wilderness is enhanced by spectacular views of the isles of Es Vedrà and the smaller Es Vedranell, two rocky sentinels opposite the 18th-century **Torre des Savinar** watchtower. Just inland are the **Ses Païses de Cala d'Hort**, excavated remains of a Carthaginian settlement dating back to the 5th century BC and later occupied by the Romans.

On the west coast leading up towards the bay of Sant Antoni are some of the finest beaches on the island. Water sports enthusiasts dispute the respective merits of **Cala Bassa**, **Cala Vedella**, **Cala Tárida** and **Cala Comte**, but each has something special to offer. At these coves you can enjoy clean, crystal-clear water and gently sloping white sandy beaches. There are good road connections between Sant Antoni and both Cala Tárida and Cala Vedella, with the result that both bays have now been developed. You can also reach Cala Bassa and Cala Comte by road (with a good bus service) or by boat. The combination of red and greyish rocks, white sands, green pines and deep blue sky and sea is striking. Local kids love exploring the nearby caves.

Past the small coves north of Sant Antoni, the rest of the coastal circle is something of a no man's land of choppy seas and razor-sharp rocks. Only one real road leads to the coast in this whole quadrant. The beach of **Port de Sant Miquel**, which once had the Arabic name of Balansat, is a deep inlet with white sand and pine woods, set far below and beyond the hilltop town of Sant Miquel. One side of the inlet has been taken over by sleek, modern hotels, but their guests seem to prefer their own swimming pools to Sant Miquel beach.

In addition to walking in the wooded hills, one of the most popular local attractions is the **Cova de Can Marçà**, a cave where sound and light effects enhance the natural wonders of stalagmites and stalactites.

FORMENTERA

Ibiza's tiny neighbour is a world apart. Less than four nautical miles away – half an hour by hydrofoil and an hour by ferry *(see page 118)* – the island of Formentera beckons to those seeking a quieter life. It has long, sandy beaches as well as easy terrain in the interior for riding bicycles or scooters. Formentera has no airport, nor are there any plans to build one. It has a sizeable salt lake but no fresh water. Cisterns, some of them dating from Arab times, catch whatever rain falls, and supplementary water supplies are shipped in when needed to this desert island.

The grandiose cliff-top views of Port de Sant Miquel are irresistible to photographers.

Potential water shortages have not been enough to stop the developers, however, and hotel complexes and scores of new apartment blocks line the beaches of Es Pujols, Platja de Migjorn, Es Caló and Cala Saona. These centres attract most of the tourists and summer residents, who swell the permanent population of roughly 5,000 to 20,000 or more. The impact of this seasonal influx of tourists (mainly German, British and French) has been dramatic. Still, there's room to spare on Formentera.

Constrained by the limited water supply and the absence of an airport, the pace of construction and change has been kept within reasonable bounds. For example, buildings are not allowed to rise higher than four storeys. Traffic has also been controlled – if you're staying here, a bicycle is the best way to explore an island that measures no more than 20km (12 miles) from end to end, one-fifth the size of Ibiza. For day-trippers, however, the best option is to rent a car or moped. Although the island is small, it is too large to see in one day by bicycle. Don't rely on public transport, either, because bus services are extremely limited.

But many visitors prefer to linger in Formentera for more than a day. They're attracted by the sun and sea, by the incomparable beaches, and by some of the finest windsurfing and scuba diving in the Mediterranean. Beautiful sandy beaches (like Platja de Migjorn) go on for miles. Nude bathing is allowed, officially, only on the isolated beaches of Ses Illetas and Llevant, but it is practised virtually everywhere, and going topless is acceptable on all the beaches. Generally speaking, people are left free to sunbathe as they please.

For all Formentera's happy-go-lucky ways, traditions are still firmly entrenched. Farmers continue, as precariously as ever, to scratch a living from the arid, rocky soil. Wheat, barley and oats are the most significant crops despite the lack of freshwater sources. Wheat, in fact, has been cultivated since Roman times, when the island was known as Frumenteria, or 'wheat producer'. Other crops include the grapes used for Formentera's distinctive dry red wine *(vino de pagés)*. Almond and fig trees thrive, but the olive trees here bear little fruit.

Life still revolves around stucco farmhouses with tiled roofs and columned verandas. Lush, red tomatoes, threaded in garlands, hang from the rafters while almonds are shelled and sold to tourists, together with

The stark parish church dominates the centre of Sant Françesc de Formentera

honey and figs. You'll also find the results of an industrious winter's knitting: gloves, scarves, caps, socks and pullovers fashioned from coarse, cream-coloured, homespun wool. No matter how enthusiastically they welcome tourism, the islanders seem reluctant to abandon a rural lifestyle, and this further enhances the local charm.

Island Sights

From Eivissa, ferries and hydrofoils heading for Formentera pass the privately owned, uninhabited little island of **S'Espalmador**, with its lovely white-sand beach. Port d'S'Espalmador bay is popular with yachtsmen, including King Juan Carlos.

Passengers disembark onto the quayside at **La Savina**, Formentera's only port. From here you can take in at a glance the languorous activity of the harbour and the spate of construction that is changing the skyline of the town. Here, too, you can rent a car, scooter, moped, or bicycle or catch the bus. The port is the only terminal for Formentera's limited – and not too reliable – public transport system. There are also taxis available for hire here.

Follow the main road inland past the island's lone petrol station (which is closed after dark) to the town of **Sant Françesc de Formentera**, known in Castilian as San Francisco Javier. This is Formentera's main town, with a population of around 1,000. Parked at the back of the new town hall is the jaunty Land Rover that serves as a fire engine, the first on Formentera and just one of the beneficial side effects of the tourist boom.

Far de sa Mola, the 19th-century lighthouse on the edge of the cliff, with the sea far below.

The most prominent structure here is the **Església de Sant Françesc Xavier**. Squat as a bunker, this fortress of whitewashed stone sheltered townspeople when pirate raids threatened. Visitors now descend on the town's three main streets, and a growing number of souvenir shops proclaims the new order of things.

From Sant Françesc, take the road that leads southwest to Cap de Barbària (the southernmost point in the Balearic Islands). Just over 1.5km (1 mile) west of town you pass the turn-off to the small, sandy bay of **Cala Saona**, which is framed by cliffs of red rock and hotel and holiday apartment blocks. Except for this little *cala*, this part of the island is sparsely populated. There are a few farms, scattered fields marked by stone walls, and corrals enclosing sheep, goats and pigs. The parched landscape grows ever more desolate as you approach **Cap de Barbària**, and the road deteriorates until it's no more than a dusty track. The remains of three prehistoric settlements lie just off the road. The cape itself is the haunt of wild goats and the site of an isolated lighthouse and a watchtower, both built high above the sea.

After the solitary beauty of Cap de Barbària comes **Platja de Migjorn**, a sublime arc of sand 8km (5 miles) long that is extremely popular, but big enough to remain uncongested. The area has been developed with a number of hotels, notably Club Riu La Mola (Formentera's most luxurious resort), as well as a number of more low-key establishments.

Continue to the easternmost point of the island, to the village of **El Pilar de sa Mola** and **Far de sa Mola**, a lighthouse built in 1861 and still in operation. A veteran keeper lives on the premises, tending the beacon that is visible 65km (40 miles) out to sea. As a nearby monument proclaims, Far de sa Mola was featured in the Jules Verne adventure *Journey Round the Solar System*. Time and technological advances have passed the lighthouse by, but it's not difficult to see why it caught Verne's imagination. It is a splendid location, and the views are magnificent.

More glorious still is the panorama from the *mirador* above **Es Caló**, a lookout point that is one of the highest spots on the island. It stands right beside the road in full view of the narrow spine of land that connects eastern Formentera to the island's western half. The white expanse of Platja de Migjorn, clearly visible on the southern side, is paralleled by the rocky strip of beach on the Es Caló side. Es Caló's tiny harbour dates from Roman times, when it was Formentera's only port. Nearby, a Roman encampment, **Can Blai**, has recently been excavated. Today Es Caló is yet another target for tourist development, and there are already several small hotels and apartment complexes set among the pine woods.

After Es Caló, go northwest along the main trans-island road to **Sant Ferran**, a pleasant village with a pretty church. It had its brief moment of glory in the late 1960s as the rendezvous for American and European hippies. The bar at Fonda Pepe *(see page 132)* claims to have served drinks to Bob Dylan. The nearby **Covas d'en Xeroni** (open daily 10am–8pm), with stalagmites and stalactites, can be visited.

Head north back to the coast and **Es Pujols**, Formentera's main resort, where scores of bars, restaurants and kiosks cater to tourists. On the nearest beach, Platja de Pujols, you can scarcely see the sand during peak season for the sun-loungers, sunbaked bodies, pedalos and windsurfing gear. Farther north, the beaches of **Ses Illetes** (the official nude beach) and Platja de Llevant are quieter. Don't expect too much in the way of facilities, though; these simple establishments are intended to be dismantled at the end of every season, when the area returns to blessed tranquillity.

The oldest construction on Formentera, a prehistoric stone circle of dolmen megaliths, lies not far north of Es Pujols, between La Savina road and Formentera's salt lake, at **Ca Na Costa**. The Bronze Age site is still under excavation but is open to the public at all hours. A shelter has been erected to protect the limestone pillars from the elements.

Also here is Formentera's salt-reclaiming area, **Ses Salines**. To reach the salt lake, follow the road on the outskirts of La Savina before turning right (eastwards) down a rough lane, at the end of which you turn left.

First utilised in Roman times, the salt pans today are the source of 18,000 metric tons (20,000 tons) of salt each year. The salt has large crystals, with a higher density than that from Ibiza, and is considered excellent for curing fish. The export point, of course, is La Savina, the first and last port of call on any trip round the island.

Formentera's beginnings – a prehistoric circle of dolmens at Ca Na Costa.

Island Flora

The rewards of a close-up look at the countryside of Ibiza include a botanical treasury. If you're interested in plants and flowers and want to know what's in bloom when, here's a calendar.

January Mimosa bushes are covered with yellow puffballs.

February A blizzard of white and pink almond blossom is unforgettable. On the hills giant blue irises, yellow gorse and tiny bee orchids create an impressionist landscape.

March–April Fields of daisies – even daisy bushes – and pink field gladioli announce spring on Ibiza.

May–June The striking scarlet of flowering pomegranate trees contrasts with the red of poppies in the cornfields and with the bright yellow flowers of the prickly pear.

July–August Now the garden flowers bloom: honeysuckle in yellow and cream; the blue, trumpet-shaped morning glory; and pink and white oleander. Bougainvillaea starts to sprout bright green leaves and scarlet flowers. Even when you're on the beach, flowers are not far away, with sweet-scented sea daffodils pushing up out of the sand.

September Rainbows of petunias, geraniums and dahlias appear. Look out for the white spikes of the yucca plant.

October The prickly pear is laden with yellow and purple fruit; tiny narcissus and merendera flower after the first autumn rains; and you can enjoy the brown and yellow zinnias.

November In shady woods, white and pink heather hugs the ground, while rosemary bushes, covered with tiny blue flowers, dot open areas.

December Orange and lemon trees bear fruit.

Almost the year round in the most unexpected places – in tiny crevices between rocks, alongside every road and path – the wildflowers, sometimes almost microscopic, offer a wild bouquet of colour and life.

The island's colourful flora is a joy for nature lovers all year round.

WHAT TO DO

SPORTS AND OUTDOOR ACTIVITIES

Water sports are the natural first choice on two islands that enjoy year-round sunshine and a sea that is nearly always warm. Whether you favour diving, sailing, windsurfing or simply swimming, you will be faced with plenty of choices. All these aquatic activities have been enhanced in recent years by the considerable efforts of local authorities to keep coastal waters unpolluted.

But there is more to Ibiza and Formentera than beaches. There are plenty of wilderness trails for hikers, mountain-bikers and horse riders wishing to explore the interior or the clifftop paths. And there are also limitless opportunities for those who want to relax and do nothing at all. The fine white sands or smooth pebbles make ideal day-beds for lazing in the sun. Lazing is such a perfect pastime that some visitors never get around to reading the fat paperback they bought at the airport. The role models seem to be the islands' lizards, who know exactly how to behave in the sun. However, most visitors rouse themselves sufficiently to do a little shopping for local products in the island towns and markets.

Whatever you are doing, you should be wary of the Mediterranean sun – and not just during the summer months. You'll get a suntan without working at it, even if you spend only half an hour in the morning and another half hour in the late afternoon sunbathing. Ultraviolet rays operate even in the shade, and the sun bounces off the water, the wet rocks and the white walls. Wear a hat and a T-shirt for protection, use a strong sunscreen and remember that you can burn when you are in the water. Don't forget to drink lots of water, too.

Watersports

Boating and sailing. The yacht clubs and many of the beach resorts have sailing boats for hire and some also give lessons. Rates are not at all prohibitive – in fact, they are often cheaper than in mainland Spanish resorts.

Sailing boats. Suitable for a crew of two, these are just the ticket if you want to learn to sail. Beach bars and most water sports schools hire sailing boats. Instruction is optional, but lessons are advisable for real novices.

Motor boats. Local officials rigidly enforce the Spanish law stipulating that only captains with an official licence may operate motor boats. Consequently, these craft are seldom available for hire to tourists without a skipper.

Pedalos. These popular two-seat contraptions are sufficiently stable for a young child accompanied by an adult. They are also perfect as a personalised ferry to reach coves for snorkelling or just to avoid the crowds.

A windsurfer catching a breeze off Formentera has no time to admire Ibiza in the background.

Plain sailing – just enjoy the rugged coastline as you drift through clear waters.

Windsurfing. Windsurfing is a major attraction on Ibiza and Formentera – far more so than water-skiing these days. Equipment can be hired and lessons taken at a number of windsurfing schools *(escuelas de windsurfing)* in many of the resorts *(see page 64)*.

Fishing. Catching fish along the rocky coastline is a popular pursuit, no matter how unlikely the prospect of a large haul. For deep-sea fishing, contact the premier charter company, Pesca Ibiza, Edificio Brisol 2, Avinguda 8 Agosto, Eivissa, tel: 971 314 491.

Scuba diving and snorkelling. The waters off Ibiza and Formentera are wonderfully clear and perfect for diving; they are ideal for both experienced divers and those who want to learn from scratch. It is essential to note that spearfishing with scuba equipment is strictly forbidden. Also, the shores of Ibiza contain so much archaeological treasure that the government keeps a sharp eye on all divers. Before you can dive underwater, you must have a licence from the CRIS (Centro de Recuperación y Investigaciones Submárinas, or Underwater Recovery and Research Centre). Registered diving schools will be able to help you with the formalities as well as telling you where to find the most interesting wrecks *(see page 64)*.

Snorkelling equipment is relatively cheap in the shops, but test the face mask carefully before you buy it. With a little practice, almost anyone can find an interesting rock formation and watch the multicoloured fish pass in review. Snorkel fishing with spear guns is legal, but the fish (which can often be frisky with unarmed snorkellers) now know to scatter at the sight of a harpoon.

If you don't feel squeamish about it, you can prowl the rocks in shallow waters with a mask and spear in search of squid. These tentacled creatures might look terrible under water, but out in the air they're revealed as small and not at all dangerous. In winter, thousands of squid lurk among the rocks in very shallow waters along the coast, and the only equipment you need to catch them is a face mask and *gancho* (hook). The problem is learning how to distinguish between the squid and the rocks they settle in. If you can solve that one, you'll have a lot of fun as well as a few catches.

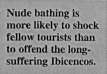

Nude bathing is more likely to shock fellow tourists than to offend the long-suffering Ibicencos.

Swimming. Most Ibiza hotels and apartment complexes have their own freshwater pools. On Formentera, however, this is not always the case. However, the sea is usually so warm and inviting that a pool is not a necessity on either island *(see page 41 for the best beaches)*. Deck chairs, sun loungers and umbrellas can be hired on most beaches.

The concept of a professional lifeguard is practically unknown on Ibiza and Formentera. However, most of the favourite beaches are well protected from waves and undertow, and they have a very gradual slope. Normally they are safe, but be sure to take care on a rough day. *(For the safest beaches for children, see page 41.)* Some beach bars keep first aid supplies to help with superficial problems.

Diving and Watersports Schools

Aigua Viva (Santa Eulària, tel: 971 302 595) offers diving and windsurfing lessons and facilities.

Anfibios (Platja d'en Bossa, tel: 971 192 418) runs courses for beginners and offers trips and equipment for experienced divers.

César Centro Deportivo Náutico (Platja s'Argamassa, tel: 971 330 919) specialises in sailing and water skiing.

Ibiza Diving (Puerto Deportivo, Santa Eulària, tel: 971 332 949) caters for newcomers and seasoned divers.

Vellmari (Avinguda del Mediterani, La Savina, Formentera, tel: 971 322 105) is a reputable diving school.

Wet Four Fun (Roca Plana, Es Pujols, tel: 971 321 809) is a sailing and windsurfing centre that also organises activities for children.

Donkey Treks

More than 50 trained donkeys work at the *burro* ranch near Santa Gertrudis. An outing from here includes a 20-minute ride over a mountain followed by a wine-tasting party. Watch out for the donkey that drinks *sangría* from a *porrón*, which is quite a feat. The combination of the scenery, the ride and the general fun and games makes this a very popular excursion. Many travel agencies offer donkey trek excursions, but if you choose to drive to Santa Gertrudis on your own it will cost you about half as much.

Using donkeys for leisure purposes is a recent development. *Burros* have been used as beasts of burden since the time of the ancient Egyptians. Those big-eared, sure-footed creatures can still be found on farms all over Ibiza, gainfully employed in spite of competition from tractors and trucks.

Sports on Land

For those weary of water, there is plenty to do on land. Once again, however, remember to be careful in the sun.

Tennis. There are no grass courts on the islands, but a number of asphalt courts are available at hotels and apartment complexes. Courts can be hired by the hour, usually with advance booking. A few hotels offer professional coaching; prices vary according to the reputation of the teacher. Also try Club de Tenis de Santa Eulària, tel: 971 331 499; or Tennis Club, Carrer Canaries, Eivissa, tel: 971 300 019.

Golf and miniature golf. An unexpected sight, in a remote valley near Cala Llonga, is a meticulously tended golf course, El Club de Golf de Ibiza, Roca Llisa, tel: 971 196 118. Those who feel a holiday isn't the same without a game are welcome to tee off there. Or try the smaller Club Terra Nova, Ctra Cala Llonga, Km 10, Santa Eulària, tel: 971 338 135. There's also miniature golf available in Sant Antoni, Santa Eulària, or Portinatx on Ibiza, and at Club Riu La Mola on quieter Formentera.

Hiking and biking. These are two ideal ways of getting off the beaten track and away from the madding crowd. Bikes can be hired in most towns and resorts. The newly environmentally-conscious tourist authorities provide Green Tours trail maps and descriptions of the countryside and sights along your route. Trails are signposted with the island's emblem: Eleonora's falcon. The pamphlets grade the trails according to difficulty. Most of the cycling routes on Ibiza are quite long and some can be arduous; those on Formentera are shorter. But there are plenty of walking routes to suit people of all ages and abilities. Aigua Viva, Santa Eulària, tel: 971 302 595, hires mountain bikes and offers advice on hiking (*senderismo*), alongside its range of aquatic activities.

Wear sensible walking shoes and take a hat for protection against the sun; pack drinking water and a torch to light the way back from a sunset view. When part of the route coincides with a normal road, remember that pedestrians should walk on the left.

Horse riding and horse racing. The countryside of Ibiza, with its gentle green hills and grid of fairly quiet back roads, is perfectly suited to horse riding. A few recognised riding stables are: Centro Equestre Easy-Rider, Cala Llonga, tel: 971 196 511; Rancho Can Dog, Ctra Sant Juan, Km 14, tel: 971 325 284; Rancho Can Mayans, Ctra Santa Gertrudis, tel: 971 187 388; Rancho Can Puig, Santa Gertrudis, tel: 607 144 029. At Ponylandia, Cta Eivissa–Jesús, tel: 630 204 272, there are pony rides for children.

The terracotta ceramics of Sant Rafel have centuries of tradition behind them and make wonderful souvenirs.

Horse racing and trotting takes place, usually on Tuesday and Saturday evening, at the Hipódromo Ibiza, Sant Rafel, tel: 971 198 191, and on Sunday at the Hipódromo Sant Jordi Cta Eivissa–Aeropuerto, tel: 971 396 669. The race courses are also put to other uses: Sant Jordi regularly stages a big second-hand market; and the Hipódromo Ibiza hosted the MTV festival in 2001.

Yoga. Ibiza has become a popular place for yoga holidays, where accommodation and daily sessions, tailored to suit beginners as well as experienced practitioners, are offered as part of a package. Contact Ibiza Yoga, Carrer Papeleria Labritja 42, Sant Joan de Labritja, tel: 971 333 557; in the UK, tel: 020 7419 0999, e-mail: info@ibizayoga.com, <www.ibizayoga.com>.

SHOPPING

Shopping hours

Strictly observing the traditional afternoon siesta, shops stay open from around 9am to 1pm and from 4pm to 8pm. The big supermarkets may open later in the morning but remain open till 10pm. Most boutiques in the resorts open only during the tourist season, from Easter till November, but they usually stay open until late in the evening.

Where to shop

The area around the port in Eivissa offers the largest choice of shops on the island. Quite a few establishments devote themselves primarily to their local customers, rather than selling tourist gear. The trendier fashion boutiques, which are of more interest to visitors, are to be found in La Marina and up in Dalt Vila. Shops in Passeig Vara de Rey cater more to the mass market.

Best Buys

As a rule, prices on Ibiza are slightly higher than on the Spanish peninsula, and you will find few real bargains these days.

Shoes. Shoes for both men and women can be quite cheap, but anything stylish is likely to cost as much as it would at home. Very popular are the traditional *alpargatas* or *esperdenyes de bed,* made of local *esparto* straw, hemp, and white *pita* fibre at heel and toe. They are ideal for the beach, for shopping, or for lounging around at the hotel. You will probably throw them away when you're ready to leave. For good quality, made to measure leather sandals, go to the Sandal Shop, Plaça de la Vila, Eivissa, tel: 971 305 475.

A pharmacy or chemist's is called a *farmacia* (fahr-mah-thee-ah). They are very efficient, and concentrate on pharmaceutical products – they don't sell film, cosmetics, toilet articles, books or newspapers.

Bags. Another perennial favourite, useful and inexpensive, is the voluminous straw shoulder bag for shopping or carrying beach equipment. Popular with both islanders and visitors, they come in various sizes, for children and adults. Over the years these bags have proved so handy that, to keep up with demand, the local supply of genuine hand-made bags has been augmented with imported goods.

Jewellery. Gold and silver jewellery, made on the spot or elsewhere in Spain, is popular for both quality and price. You will also see hippie jewellery (mostly Mexican- or Indian-style silver) on sale, especially at the markets in Punta Arabí (Wednesday) and Las Dalias, Sant Carles (Saturday). Some of the artisans here look as if they are straight out of the 1960s themselves. Haggling over prices is quite acceptable, even if not always successful.

Clothing. The trendy resort clothing available here – fashioned on the island by the designers of the Ad Lib group, which began in the mid-1970s – has a cachet all of its own. Selling from Manhattan to Tokyo, styles change each season, but the trademark 'biza look' remains light and airy, with a loose cut and bright colours setting off the basic Ibicenco white. Contact the Fashion Association of Ibiza, Avinguda Espanya 18, Eivissa, tel: 971 302 911 for details of official Ad Lib designers.

Pottery. The terracotta bowls of Sant Rafel and Sant Josep have centuries of tradition behind them. Many of the patterns and forms still show a medieval Arab influence. Artesanía de Ibiza, Carrer Isidor Macabich 34, Santa Eulària has some interesting, good-quality items. Be careful what you choose: inadequately fired, unglazed pottery is risky to ship or pack and outdoor pots are not frost-proof.

Lines of earthenware vases, urns, bowls, and pots – you name it, they can throw it.

Alcohol and tobacco. Both products are inexpensive compared with European and American prices. Imported Cuban cigars, plentiful and cheap, are a favourite present to take home, although they are still outlawed by US Customs. While foreign-brand alcohol, produced under licence in Spain, sells for just a few euros a bottle, there are more unusual local spirits that might make apt souvenirs. *Hierbas* are an island speciality, liqueurs spiced with the island's wild herbs, mostly thyme, known as *frigola*. *Anís seco* or *anís dulce* are dry or sweet aniseed-based spirits. Bodegas Ribas, Carrer Sant Vicent, Santa Eulària, has the widest choice of *hierbas* and wines.

Local foods. Island foods and Spanish imports are good things to take home and are often much appreciated as gifts. Almonds, olives, olive oil, chorizo and salami-type sausage, cheese, almond biscuits and dried figs are all worth buying. Look for these items in the picturesque open-air market of Sa Penya (Eivissa) or, for a wider selection, at the bustling, covered central market in the newer part of town (Carrer d'Extremadura).

Barbecues

A popular excursion organised by tour agencies is the all-you-can-eat-and-drink barbecue outing. You will arrive at a rustic setting where meat is sizzling over glowing coals and unlimited quantities of red wine or *sangría* are waiting to be drunk. Following the feast, a band usually plays music for dancing.

You'll learn to drink wine from a *porrón*, a glass container with a pointed spout from which the liquid arcs through the air into your open mouth – in theory, anyway. To enjoy the experience fully, don't wear your best clothes and remember to put a napkin around your neck.

Antiques. In the past there must have been intriguing opportunities to buy up Ibicenco antiques and ship them home. Today it would take more time seeking them out than the average visitor is willing to invest. Browse around the shops, however, and you might find an appealing piece of old ironwork or hand carving. There are several places worth checking out in Eivissa and Santa Gertrudis. Two long-standing ones are Galeria Can Daifa, off Plaça del Església, Santa Gertrudis; and Vivian Scott, Carrer Jaume 1, Eivissa.

ENTERTAINMENT

The Folk Culture of Ibiza

In Spain's post-Franco revival of authentic regional culture, Ibicenco folk singing and dancing became recognised as exuberant art forms that are unique to the island. Regular shows take place in villages such as Sant Miquel and Sant Josep. There are often special one-off performances in other towns and villages during fies-

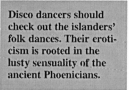

Disco dancers should check out the islanders' folk dances. Their eroticism is rooted in the lusty sensuality of the ancient Phoenicians.

tas, which usually celebrate local saints' days and other religious festivals *(see page 73 for the major festivals)*. Getting to these events is usually easier and cheaper if you go on one of the excursions organised in all the resorts.

The colourful, traditional costume for men includes the red hats, called *barretinas*, bandanas tied round the neck, gold-trimmed black corduroy or cotton jackets over loose-fitting, high-collared white shirts, bright red cummerbunds, baggy trousers of white linen (wide at the thighs but tight at the ankles) and an open, toeless version of the familiar Ibicenco straw *alpargata* shoes.

Islanders wear lavish traditional dress when celebrating fiestas.

The costume worn by the women is more lavish. It includes a long, pleated skirt of homespun wool, either black or white; an elaborately patterned apron; a fine silk shawl with long-tassells that is worn over the shoulders and a large lace mantilla over the head. Hair is braided down the back and sometimes tied with a schoolgirl ribbon. Around the neck hang a heavy golden necklace, ribbons, a gold scapular with images of saints on both sides and a crucifix.

Much of this adornment – such as the *emprendad* necklace – is gold filigree of Arab design. In addition, the women wear various heavy rings. The clothing is so original and ornate that a fair amount of time is spent at each folklore show explaining it in detail. Even the children wear miniature versions of these costumes.

The traditional *ball pagès* (country dances) take many forms, each portraying an often long-forgotten ritual. Most of the dances now performed suggest ancient courtship, with the man being forceful and arrogant, the woman shyly flirtatious. In one dance, the women form a circle, moving in small steps, their eyes cast down, while the men, outside the circle, seek to attract their attention with ostentatious high kicks. Often the songs have witty, ribald lyrics, inevitably watered down in the impromptu translation.

The music is played on typically Catalan – and in some cases uniquely Ibicenco – instruments: a wooden flute and a small drum (handled together by one man with astonishing dexterity), a sort of steel sabre struck rhythmically, and large castanets. The music reflects unmistakable Arab roots, although over the centuries it has accumulated a number of additional elements. Some of the light-hearted songs require the singer to emit an unusual, guttural 'ye-ye-ye' sound.

Festivals

The popular *fiestas* of Ibiza are less formidable than the equivalent *ferias* of mainland Spain. Now that tourists are a primary audience, several feast days offer special events and fireworks that were never part of the original celebrations. For the visitor, the most interesting observances are the modest old standbys, generally the saint's day of a village: sober religious processions often held by candle light, with folk music and an array of quaint costumes.

In the following list we describe the annual festivals held on fixed or regular dates. Check with the tourist office *(see page 121)* for information about other events.

mid-February *Carnaval* (Carnival), Santa Eulària: celebrations also held in other parts of the island.

First Sunday in May *Festa Floral* (Flower Festival), Santa Eulària: a spring celebration with decorated wagons.

23–24 June *Nit de Sant Joan* (St John the Baptist), Eivissa, Sant Antoni and La Mola, Formentera: fireworks, bonfires, craft markets and festivities. This is an important holiday, and the time when Ibicenco landowners and tenant farmers make their verbal contracts for the coming year.

16 July *Virgen del Carmen* (Maritime Festival), Eivissa: regattas held in honour of the Virgin. Similar celebrations are held in La Savina, Formentera, and in Sant Antoni on the following Sunday.

25 July *Festa de Santiago* (St James), Formentera: procession, folk songs, and dancing in honour of the saint.

1–8 August *Santa Maria de las Neus* (Our Lady of the Snows), Eivissa: bands, fireworks, folk dances, sporting events and religious services honour the patron saint.

24 August *Sant Bartomeu* (St Bartholomew's Day), Sant Antoni: procession, high mass, concerts, fireworks and sporting activities.

8 September *Festa de Jésus,* Santa Eulària: a popular religious festival.

29 September *Sant Miquel* (St Michael's Day): celebrated with special panache by masterly folk dancers and musicians.

1 November *Tots Sants* (All Saints' Day), both islands: special cakes, pastries and nuts sold in markets.

3 December *Sant Francesc Xavier* (St Francis' Day), Sant Francesc de Formentera: procession, dancing, folk songs.

Nightlife

Such is the appeal of Ibiza's nightclubs that, after a couple of weeks' holiday on the island, many young people manage to leave without a suntan. And no regrets. For some, the nightlife is the only reason to come here in the first place. By day, they sleep – or dance at one of the daytime discos. Some English charter groups have been known simply to fly in for the night and go home the next day. At the last estimate Ibiza had some 80 clubs and nightspots, ranging from opulent, glowing discos (complete with elegant restaurants, multi-level cocktail bars, half a dozen dance floors and even an indoor swimming pool) to sleazy saloons with just one small dance floor. Both have their *aficionados*. The one thing they have in common is a deafening sound system.

A major island highlight is the extravagant theme evening with shows involving audience participation, ranging from beauty contests for both sexes, to communal baths in foam – or whipped cream – and fashion parades.

For many years Eivissa itself was not the place to go for the club scene; instead, it attracted only a special clientele to Dalt Vila's gay bars. Now it has two major clubs, Pacha and El Divino (the only two on the island that are open in winter), with plenty of other entertainment available. Sant Antoni can certainly still lay claim to the island's most spectacular club venues, as it has for many years, but it also features smaller clubs and bars with disc jockeys or live music of various kinds, including jazz. The Platja d'en Bossa area west of Eivissa also has a lively nightlife, with Irish bars and live music in the clubs.

Take in the broad sweep of Platja de ses Figueretes from the castle in Eivissa before party time begins.

In the summer months a Discobus service operates between the major resorts from midnight to dawn *(see Recommended Clubs, page 141, for details of current hot spots)*. Don't forget that many large hotels also offer evening activities every night of the week, and you don't need to be a guest of the hotel to participate.

Eivissa's casino, handily located on the waterfront promenade (Passeig Joan Carles I; tel: 971 313 312) is open year round, from 10pm–5am. To gain entrance to the gaming room, you must present your passport or identification papers. Then, for a small fee, you will receive a computerised admission card, good for one or more days of roulette as well as blackjack and craps. The stakes for many of the games are low, so you can try your hand without risking too much. Early in the evening, tourists crowd in for a look at what's going on but, as the night progresses, the dyed-in-the-wool gamblers gradually take over.

Ibiza has plenty of activities for children. Getting behind the wheel on a go-kart track is fun.

Also on the casino premises is a nightclub with a floor show and an excellent restaurant *(see page 134)*.

Most films in Ibiza's cinemas are Spanish, or American and British films dubbed into Spanish. As well as the conventional cinemas in Eivissa, other places that show films on the island are old-fashioned, sometimes picturesque. Once or twice a week you can see films in English in both Santa Eulària and Sant Antoni (check with the tourist office).

ACTIVITIES FOR CHILDREN

Children are rarely happier than when playing on a beach, and most of the beaches on Ibiza and Formentera provide safe conditions and good facilities. If the beach gets boring, take the kids out on a pedalo or a glass-bottomed boat. What they spot below the boat is likely to whet the appetite of some of the older children for snorkelling.

When choosing your hotel, check on the special facilities many of them provide for children's activities on the beach or around the swimming pool; some have children's entertainment in the hotel as well.

Most of the riding stables scattered across the island have ponies for children. Trotting races at the two race courses are great fun for the whole family, too *(see pages 66–7)*. A leisurely way of getting around is on a donkey from the *burro* ranch near Santa Gertrudis – with *sangría* as a bonus for the parents *(see page 64)*.

There are two well-equipped water parks on Ibiza: Aguamar, Platja d'en Bossa, tel: 971 396 790/971 300 671; and Aqualandia, Cap Martinet, Talamanca, tel: 971 192 411. Both open daily from 10am–7pm throughout the summer and there are bus services from Eivissa. There are go-kart tracks in Santa Eulària and Sant Antoni; both are open daily in summer until midnight.

EATING OUT

The variety of Ibiza's cuisine reflects the island's image as a cosmopolitan resort with traditions firmly anchored in a Catalan and, even earlier, an Arabic past. There are also good quality French, Italian and other international restaurants. Ibicenco cooking can be both robust and subtle, using Spanish ham and pork from the mainland and saffron and other herbs or spices from North Africa. Marrying them together are the variations created with fish and shellfish caught in local waters or farther afield. And as an unabashed centre for mass-tourism, Ibiza also has plenty of pizzerias and casual spots for fish-and-chips, bratwürst and hamburgers.

If, with a few exceptions, Sant Antoni happily dishes out fast food, Santa Eulària is renowned for the quality of its typical Ibicenco restaurants. Bars selling tapas, the small dishes that can combine to make a whole meal, are particularly good, both in Eivissa and Santa Gertrudis. One of the best reasons for an excursion into the interior of Ibiza is to hunt down one of the many fine restaurants. Formentera is better known for the seafood taverns on the beach. *(See Recommended Restaurants, page 133 for a selection of the islands' eating establishments.)*

RESTAURANTS AND MEAL TIMES

Spanish restaurants are officially graded and awarded a rating in 'forks', from one fork to four. However, ratings are based on facilities and not on the quality of the food. Several forks might guarantee linen tablecloths and higher prices but not necessarily better food.

Spanish restaurants generally offer a set menu at a set price *(menú del día)*. This is normally three courses plus a glass of wine or beer. The *menú* is always economical if not always inspired, and is a good way to eat if you're on a budget. It is often available only at lunchtime. It is important to note that if a waiter asks '¿Menú?' he is referring to this special meal of the day. If you want to look at the actual menu and see what else is offered, then you should ask for *la carta*.

Most menu prices include taxes and some include a service charge (look for the words *servicio incluido* on the bill), but if not, it's customary to leave a tip if service was satisfactory; about 10 percent is usual. All restaurants announce that official complaint forms are available to clients.

On the Spanish mainland, late eating hours perplex some visitors: lunch hardly ever starts until 2pm, and dinner might wait till 10pm. However, on Ibiza, meals are usually eaten somewhat earlier. Restaurants serve lunch from 1– 3pm and dinner from about 8–11pm.

*Choose picnic ingredients
from among the fresh food piled up in Ibiza's markets.*

If you want to keep costs down, ask for *vino de la casa* (house wine). This will usually cost well under half the price of a labelled wine and is usually quite acceptable. All alcoholic drinks – unless you go for something like imported Scotch – are much less expensive than in the UK and the US.

Breakfast

Lunch and dinner are the major island meals and the standard Ibizan breakfast is simply a cup of coffee and a pastry. *Ensaimadas* (sweet, sugared rolls made with lard) are a Balearic speciality. Another breakfast staple is *churros* (sugared fritters), which you dip into coffee or hot chocolate.

In deference to foreign habits, most hotels and some cafés now offer a *desayuno completo* consisting of orange juice, toast and coffee, either with or without eggs. Breakfast coffee *(café con leche)* is half coffee, half hot milk. *Café solo* is a small, strong black coffee. Hot chocolate with cream is known as *un suizo,* meaning, not surprisingly, 'a Swiss'.

Beach Restaurants

Beach restaurants serving drinks and meals, or at least snacks, right at the water's edge always have a special appeal. Because they're supposed to be dismantled at the end of the season, these modest establishments are mostly somewhat makeshift, but they are nonetheless convenient and appealingly atmospheric.

Bars and Cafés

From early in the morning to late at night, during the summer season, at least, bars and cafés serve breakfast, snacks, coffee and drinks. At most open-air cafés, a cup of coffee buys you a ringside seat for as long as you care to linger; no one will rush you. One of the few exceptions is in Sant Antoni, where some cafés refuse to serve coffee at all during peak hours, preferring the higher profits from alcohol.

Wines and spirits are served at all hours in Spain. Children are welcome in most bars and often accompany their parents on late-night outings, having recouped their energy during a siesta.

Bar and café bills include service, but small tips are the custom. It usually costs 20 percent less to sit at the bar for a coffee or a drink than to be served at a table.

Sit at an outdoor café and watch the world go by.

Note that *cafeterías* are not the self-service restaurants that you might expect. Instead, they are glorified snack bars. The word originally meant a café, but the range of service has been expanded to include full meals.

Bodegas are wine cellars. On the mainland, many popular tourist bars have been designed to recreate the atmosphere of a traditional wine cellar. However, on Ibiza a *bodega* is usually a wholesale and retail wine store rather than a place to sit and try the vintages. Prices are reasonable.

Tapas bars offer an alternative to a formal meal in a restaurant. These bars have spread all over Europe, so everyone now knows that tapas are small portions of food – meatballs, olives, fried fish, prawns, chorizo, etc. The word *tapa* itself means lid and derives from the old custom of offering a free,

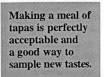

Making a meal of tapas is perfectly acceptable and a good way to sample new tastes.

bite-sized morsel of food with a drink, served on a saucer sitting on top of the glass, like a lid. Today, sadly, the custom of giving away tapas has gone, but the custom of eating them is stronger than ever. You can wander into a tapas bar, point to the items you like, and eat your way down the counter, rather like a smorgasbord. One helping is called a *porción;* a large serving is a *ración,* and half as much is a *media ración.* It is worth learning these terms, as you can easily order more food than you need and spend more than for a conventional meal.

WHAT TO EAT

Spanish Specialities

Gazpacho (pronounced 'gath-*pat*-cho') is an Andalusian invention, a chilled soup, based on oil, bread and garlic, to which chopped cucumbers, peppers, tomatoes, onions and croutons are added to taste. Aptly described as 'liquid salad', it can be a very refreshing meal.

Paella ('pie-*ale*-ya') crossed the sea to Ibiza from Valencia. It is named after the flat iron pan in which it is cooked. Among the ingredients added to saffron rice are morsels of squid and shrimp, mussels, rabbit, sausage, peppers, chicken, onions, peas and beans, tomatoes, garlic… and whatever else happens to inspire the cook.

Classically, *paella* should be served only at lunchtime and always cooked to order. It takes more than half an hour, time enough to pacify your hunger with another dish for which Spain is well known: *tortilla española* (Spanish omelette), which has no connection with Mexican tortillas. It contains potatoes and onions, is less fluffy than a French-style omelette, and usually served cold, sliced like a cake.

Fish comes from all over the Mediterranean and the Atlantic, so what you are served may be the frozen variety, rather than that freshly caught in Ibizan waters. Waiters will usually tell you if you ask. It is usually served grilled, accompanied by a salad and fried potatoes. The local catch of the day is frequently *pez espada* (swordfish) and comes as a satisfying grilled steak. Alternatively, try *salmonete* (red mullet), *mero* (grouper), or *lenguado* (sole).

In season you can find delicious varieties of shellfish, from *langostinos* (crayfish) to *gambas* (prawns) and *mejillones* (mussels). And don't forget *calamares* – squid, most commonly cut in small strips and fried in batter *(a la romana),* making either a snack or a meal in itself.

By the way, a menu's rather grand sounding *filete de pescado a la romana con patatas fritas* is just the Spanish way of saying fish and chips.

Calamares

If you're out fishing, you might catch a squid, and everyone in sight will congratulate you and advise you how to cook and eat your catch. Or you might simply buy one at the market and pretend you have caught it.

The simplest method is to simmer the squid in its own ink. Otherwise, hang it up on a line until the sun completely dries it out (at least 12 hours), cut it up into very thin slices, grill it over open coals and then sprinkle it with lemon juice. For something along the same lines but not quite so time consuming, try a dish of *calamares a la romana* (deep-fried squid) in a local restaurant.

There's plenty of meat on the menu as well: local pork and lamb, fowl and game. If you prefer a steak, you can often choose from *chateaubriand, tornedos* and *entrecôte.* The most tender cut, similar to filet mignon, is called *solomillo (filete).*

Ibizan Specialities

The local cuisine makes much use of olive oil, red wine, cereals and the island's herbs: fennel, laurel (bay leaves), basil, oregano, thyme, marjoram and mint. Since Phoenician times, islanders have used the local salt to preserve fish. After Arab irrigation methods enabled the cultivation of rice, green vegetables, citrus fruits and saffron, the Catalans brought in the custom of frying onions, tomatoes, red peppers and garlic in oil. Below are descriptions of just a few typical dishes.

Sopas: tasty, cheap soups of lentils, rice, butter beans and green beans, as well as *sopa de pescado* (fish soup) or *sopa marinera* (seafood soup).

Ibiza's excellent, home-grown fruit and vegetables add colour to a local market.

Garbanzos: chickpeas served Ibicenco-style with parsley, oil and garlic.

Sobrasada: classical Balearic pork sausage, seasoned with sweet peppers.

Butifarrons: spicy blood sausage.

Sofrit pagès (country stew): this hearty meat, sausage and potato dish is properly cooked in a broth of chicken and lamb, with saffron, garlic, sweet pepper, cinnamon and cloves.

Frita pagesa (country fry): beef, lamb or pork chops and pork liver fried with garlic, mushrooms, red pepper and potatoes.

Guisat de peix (fish stew): Ibiza's lusty answer to the French bouillabaisse, an assortment of fish with all the Mediterranean spices, plus a distinctive touch of cinnamon.

Tonyina a l'eivissenca: a tuna delicacy with pine kernels, raisins, eggs, spices, lemon juice and white wine.

Dulces: sweets, the great Ibizan weakness, from typical Balearic sweet breakfast rolls *(ensaimadas)* to *graixonera,* a kind of bread pudding, and *flaó,* a tart made with fresh goat's cheese and

> **'Enjoy your meal!'**
> *¡Buen provecho!*
> (bwayn pro-baych-oh)

mint. *Macarrones de San Juan* turns out to be macaroni cooked in sweetened milk and cinnamon. *Oreietes* are ear-shaped pies flavoured with aniseed.

The fresh local fruit is delicious. After a large lunch on a hot day, choose grapes from the nearby vines – cooling in a bowl of water – or select apricots, figs, peaches, or a ripe melon. In the right season, you can enjoy a bowl of fresh strawberries and cream *(fresas con nata),* widely advertised by the island's restaurants and cafés.

WHAT TO DRINK

The most famous of all Spanish wines is, of course, sherry *(vino de Jerez),* a wine fortified with brandy. You will find two principal types: *fino* and *oloroso*. *Fino* is a dry sherry, pale in colour with a rich bouquet. *Manzanillas* and *amontillados* belong in this category. Any *fino* will make a good apéritif.

An *oloroso,* on the other hand, is a heavy, dark dessert wine that is sweetened before being sold. Brown and cream sherries are *olorosos,* and so is an *amoroso,* though it's medium dry and pale in colour. An *oloroso* is a good after-dinner drink.

For an adequate table wine, try one of the many unpretentious wines that come from mainland Spain or Mallorca. These unsung yet worthy vintages very often cost little more than bottled mineral water. In contrast, some of the well-known Spanish wines can be quite expensive but, for many palates, not necessarily better. On rare occasions you might find a restaurant serving *vino de pagès* (local red

Quenching a Thirst

In the Balearic Islands wine is often drunk from a *porrón*, a communal container made of pottery or glass. With its wide mouth and long tapering spout, it looks more like a watering can than a drinking vessel. You fill it at the top and drink the wine from the spout; the stylised shape is traditional. The version for water (which is drunk the same way) is called a *cántaro*. During the heat of the day workmen will pass this around so that everyone present can drink their fill.

The technique isn't easy to master: tilt the container until the liquid flows into your mouth in a stream, and don't touch the spout with your lips or tongue.

Tradition credits the Arabs with its invention. Apparently they were inspired by the Prophet's dictum that wine should not be allowed to touch a Muslim's lips.

wine). Islanders often drink this somewhat acid wine mixed with lemonade *(gaseosa).*

If you don't want wine with your meal, have no qualms about ordering something else – beer, mineral water, or a soft drink. Young islanders often prefer beer to wine, and at lunchtime some older people consider wine off-limits – it's just too relaxing.

Spanish brandy has a less delicate taste than French cognac, and you might find it too heavy for your liking. It can be very cheap, often the same price as a soft drink. Relatively more expensive brands, such as Carlos I or Carlos III, are much smoother.

Sangría is a popular thirst-quenching refresher, especially in summer. Made from a mixture of red wine, lemon and orange juice and peel, brandy and mineral water with ice, it may strike you as too heavy to be consumed with a meal, and the brandy makes it a lot more powerful than the taste suggests. When you do try *sangría,* make sure it's freshly made.

A word about prices: if you insist on sticking to imported Scotch or bourbon, expect to pay a relative fortune. However, a wide range of familiar spirits and liqueurs, made under licence in Spain, as well as indigenous ones, are available at startlingly low prices.

Ibiza is proud of its own native liqueurs. The most widely seen is *hierbas* (which means, literally, herbs). This sweet potion is often a home-made product, blended with herbs and sold in old bottles. It costs less, and frequently tastes better, in the more remote areas. The syrupy *hierbas* ('ee-ayr-has') can be sipped before or after meals. During hot weather, islanders drink it with ice.

Frigola, a sweet digestive drink, good with ice, is a thyme-based commercially bottled version of *hierbas.*

Two aromatic aniseed drinks are also produced locally. Beware, though, because these colourless liquids have a considerable kick. *Anís dulce* is sweet, *anís seco* is dry and dangerously potent. These resemble French *pastis,* Greek *ouzo,* or Turkish *raki.* Ibizans like their *anís* neat. Foreign drinkers, not brought up on this custom, usually prefer to dilute *anís* with a generous splash of water. *Palo,* a slightly bitter aniseed drink that is dark brown in colour, tastes best in a long, tall glass with the addition of gin or soda and ice.

To help you order and for more information on wining and dining in Ibiza, we recommend the *Berlitz Spanish–English/English–Spanish Phrase Book and Dictionary* or the *Berlitz European Menu Reader.*

When in Ibiza, start your morning the way local people do, with an ensaimada.

To Help You Order (in Spanish)

Could we have a table?	**¿Nos puede dar una mesa?**
Do you have a set menu?	**¿Tiene un menú del día?**
I'd like a/an/some …	**Quisiera …**

beer	**una cerveza**	milk	**leche**
bread	**pan**	mineral water	**agua mineral**
coffee	**un café**	napkin	**una servilleta**
cutlery	**los cubiertos**	salad	**una ensalada**
fish	**pescado**	sandwich	**un bocadillo**
fruit	**fruta**	sugar	**azúcar**
glass	**un vaso**	tea	**un té**
meat	**carne**	(iced) water	**agua (fresca)**
menu	**la carta**	wine	**vino**

…and Read the Menu

albóndigas	**meatballs**	lenguado	**sole**
almejas	**baby clams**	manzana	**apple**
anchoas	**anchovies**	mariscos	**shellfish**
angulas	**baby eels**	mejillones	**mussels**
arroz	**rice**	melocotón	**peach**
atún	**tunny (tuna)**	merluza	**hake**
bacalao	**salt cod**	naranja	**orange**
besugo	**sea bream**	pescadilla	**whiting**
boquerones	**marinaded anchovies**	pez espada	**swordfish**
		queso	**cheese**
caballa	**mackerel**	pimientos	**peppers**
cerdo	**pork**	piña	**pineapple**
chorizo	**spicy pork sausage**	plátano	**banana**
		pollo	**chicken**
cordero	**lamb**	postre	**dessert**
dorada	**gilthead bream**	pulpo	**octopus**
entremeses	**hors-d'oeuvre**	salchichón	**salami**

HANDY TRAVEL TIPS

An A–Z Summary of Practical Information

A

ACCOMMODATION *(alojamiento)*

Accommodation in the Balearic Islands ranges from the simple but clean rooms in a *pensión* (guest house) to the more luxurious surroundings of a resort hotel. The majority of visitors to Ibiza travel with package tour operators who arrange accommodation for you. If you're travelling independently it is wise to book well in advance, as accommodation does get block booked. The room price usually, but not always, includes breakfast. In the off-season, rates are lower and vacancies easier to find, but between November and March many hotels close.

Self-catering packages offering furnished apartments or villas, instead of hotel rooms, are popular. The cost is often little more than the scheduled air fare alone, but arrangements usually need to be made well in advance.

a single/double room	**una habitación sencilla/doble**
with bath and toilet/shower	**con baño/ducha**
What's the rate per night?	**¿Cuál es el precio por noche?**
Is there a reduction for children?	**¿Hay algún descuento para los niños?**
That's too expensive.	**Eso es demasiado caro.**

AIRPORT *(aeropuerto)*

Both international and domestic flights use Ibiza's Es Codolar airport, about 9km (5 miles) south of Eivissa. If no luggage carts are available, porters will carry your bags the few steps to the taxi rank or bus stop, and should be tipped. Souvenir shops, tourist information offices, car hire counters, and currency exchanges operate here, as well as a duty-free shop – no longer applicable to citizens of European Union countries. Between 7.30am and 10.30pm an hourly bus service links the airport with the centre of Eivissa, a 15-minute journey (€1.50). Taxis make the trip in about 10 minutes (around €10). Formentera has no airport but is linked with Ibiza by a ferry service *(see page 118)*.

Porter!	**¡Mozo!**
Taxi!	**¡Taxi!**
Where's the bus for…?	**¿Dónde está el autobús para…?**

B

BICYCLE and MOTOR SCOOTER HIRE *(bicicletas/ scooters de alquiler)*

A practical and fun way to explore the islands is on two-wheeled transport that can cope with even the most narrow and bumpy paths. Bicycles can often be hired from hotels, or from the same places that hire motor scooters and mopeds, but at about a quarter of the price. Make sure you are given a puncture kit in case you get a flat tyre on a stony path. A driving licence is required when renting a scooter or moped. The use of crash helmets is compulsory in Spain when riding a motorcycle, whatever the capacity of the engine.

Where can we hire mountain bikes?	**¿Dónde alquilan bicis de montaña?**
I'd like to hire a bicycle.	**Quisiera alquilar una bicicleta.**
What's the charge per day/week?	**¿Cuánto cobran por día/ semana?**

BUDGETING FOR YOUR TRIP

Because of Ibiza's tourist boom – and because it's an island — prices of certain things tend to be higher than on mainland Spain. However, the cost of living still remains lower than in many other European countries or in North America.

How much your holiday will cost depends upon your budget and taste, but you really don't have to spend a lot to have a good time. Some prices seem topsy-turvy. In a neighbourhood bar, soft drinks, beer and Spanish brandy all cost about the same, but a bottle of mineral water might cost as much as a bottle of wine.

Transport to Ibiza. For visitors from the UK and the rest of Europe, the island is a short flight away. For a scheduled flight you can expect to pay about £250 return in peak season (mid-July to late August) and UK school half-term holidays; out of season, the price is about £160. Off-season, with a budget airline, you can find much cheaper deals; check the internet. There are also cheaper charter flights; although many are part of an inclusive package they do have seats for independent travellers; again check the internet. From the US, flights to Palma de Mallorca cost approximately $880 return, and you can get a connecting flight from there for around $100. *(See page 107 for flight details.)*

Accommodation. Hotels can be expensive relative to prices on the Spanish mainland (especially in the top categories), but most island hotels operate on a tour operator basis and package deals can be extremely reasonable. For an en suite double room in high season *(see above)* an independent traveller can expect to pay between €50 in a modest hotel and €150 in an up-market one. Rates are lower off-season. *(See Recommended Hotels, page 123.)*

Meals. Restaurant prices will be a pleasant surprise for most UK and American visitors, as even top-rated restaurants seem reasonable compared to most European cities. The Spanish institution, the *menú del día*, a fixed price midday meal, is an excellent bargain, costing around €10–15 for a 3-course meal with one drink included. In a bar, a continental breakfast (fresh orange juice, coffee and toast or croissant) will cost around €5. The average price of a three-course à la carte meal, including house wine, will be about €25–30 per person Spanish wines are an excellent deal, even in the more expensive restaurants.

Car hire. Including comprehensive insurance and tax, rates are around €35 a day with the big international companies; you get a better deal if you book for a week. There are competing local firms that will offer lower rates; and cars booked in advance via the Internet are also cheaper, approximately €180 for a week in high season *(see page 195)*.

Incidentals. Your major expenses will be excursions, entertainment and sporting activities. Organised excursions are often quite reasonably priced, and can be the best way of visiting tourist-oriented sights and attractions. Family attractions such as water parks can be quite expensive, around €13 for adults, €8 for children, but you can easily spend a whole day there, so you get your money's worth. Museum entry fees average around €2.50–€3. Golf, tennis, horse riding, windsurfing, sailing and water-skiing are all affordable compared to some other destinations, but they will add up over the course of an active holiday. Nightclub and disco covers are high (between €20 and €40), as are drinks once inside.

C

CAMPING

On Ibiza, you can camp at sites near Sant Antoni (off Ibiza Town road), at Cala Bassa (west of Sant Antoni), Cala Llonga, Punta Arabí and Es Canar (all of which are near Santa Eulària), and at Cala de Portinatx up on the north coast. If you sleep out in the open, don't stay too close to camping or caravan sites;

police responsible for the campsite might wake you to check papers. Camping is prohibited on Formentera.

May we camp here?	**¿Podemos acampar aquí?**
We have a tent/caravan (trailer).	**Tenemos una tienda de camping/una caravana.**

CAR HIRE (*coches de alquiler*)

Although the bus service is good, a car is essential if you want to get off the beaten track. Most of the big international companies are represented in Ibiza, with offices at the airport, in Eivissa and in the main resorts. There are also a number of local companies, often offering cheaper rates. Many agencies have weekly specials (all with unlimited mileage) which are very reasonable, sometimes working out as low as €25 per day. Rates are seasonal, and usually much lower out of season, and at any time if organised in advance, especially over the internet. Third-party insurance is included by law, while comprehensive insurance – *todo riesgo* – may be extra, but is well worth having. Insurance may not cover you for off-road driving, even in a four-wheel-drive vehicle. A value-added tax (IVA) of 15 percent is added to the total, but will have been included if you booked in advance.

Most types and sizes of car are available, including four-wheel-drive vehicles, but the majority are small, economy models, well suited to small parking spaces and narrow rural roads. Automatics tend to be disproportionately expensive. Hirers must be at least 21 and have held a licence for six months. You need your national driver's licence but not an international one. You usually need to give details of a major credit card as a form of deposit, but if you do not have one, some companies will ask for a refundable cash deposit plus 20 percent of the estimated hire charge paid in advance.

Ibiza and Formentera

I'd like to rent a car tomorrow.	**Quisiera alquilar un coche para mañana.**
for one day/a week	**por un día/una semana**
Please include full insurance.	**Haga el favor de incluir el seguro a todo riesgo.**

CLIMATE and CLOTHING

Climate. Ibiza is blessed with a mild climate throughout the year. Temperatures in winter, however, can be a bit cooler than in many other Spanish resorts and the nights can turn chilly in early summer and autumn, so it's best to go prepared with a sweater or light jacket. Similarly, although rain is the exception rather than the rule in summer, it can catch visitors unawares. A pack-away raincoat or umbrella is a good investment.

Ibiza enjoys a yearly average of 300 days of sunshine with a daily mean of five hours in winter and more than 10 hours in summer. Humidity is about 70 percent most of the year, rising to a high of 85 percent in August. The chart below shows monthly average temperatures for Ibiza.

	J	F	M	A	M	J	J	A	S	O	N	D
Air temperature												
°F	54	53	56	59	63	71	77	79	72	68	61	56
°C	12	12	13	15	17	22	25	26	22	20	16	13
Water temperature												
°F	56	57	57	61	67	71	76	80	73	68	65	61
°C	13	14	14	16	20	21	24	26	22	20	18	16
Days with at least 4 hours of sunshine												
	26	14	21	15	28	28	27	31	28	19	24	28

Clothing. Given Ibiza's reputation for freewheeling tolerance, it would be surprising if anyone laid down rules. Dress is informal, ranging from discreet to outlandish.

In July and August you're unlikely to need anything beyond the lightest summer clothing, day or night. At any other time of year, even when it's hot at midday, you may have to dress more warmly for cool night breezes. In the hot weather, cotton is preferable to synthetic fabrics and more comfortable.

On the beach, dressing poses little problem. Some people wear nothing at all (there's official nude bathing in certain areas) and many women go topless. When you're walking to or from the beach, slip on something casual over your swimsuit; the same goes for town wear. Less revealing clothing should, as a matter of courtesy, be worn when visiting churches. Don't go wearing a bikini top or brief shorts.

COMPLAINTS *(reclamaciones)*

Tourism is Spain's leading industry and the government takes complaints from tourists very seriously.

By law all hotels, campsites and restaurants must maintain a supply of official complaint forms *(Hoja Oficial de Reclamación/Full Oficial de Reclamació)* accessible to guests. Merely asking for this form is usually enough to resolve most matters. New legislation has been introduced that greatly strengthens the consumer's hand. Public information offices are being set up, controls carried out, and fallacious information made punishable by law. For a visitor's needs, however, the tourist office or, in really serious cases, the police, will normally be able to handle problems or advise you where to go.

CRIME and SAFETY *(crimen; robo)*

Unfortunately, even on a small island like Ibiza there has been an upsurge in petty crime. In crowded places such as markets, and at fiestas, tourists should be on the lookout for pickpockets and bag-snatchers. Be alert when getting money from cash machines (ATMS). Don't under any circumstances take any valuables to the beach or leave them on view in a car. Use your hotel safe for valuables and don't carry too much cash. It's advisable to make a photocopy of your passport details and keep it somewhere safe, in case your passport is lost.

If you lose something, check first at your hotel desk, then report the loss to the municipal police or *Guardia Civil* (Civil Guard). In order to claim on insurance, a police report, made within 24 hours of the loss or theft, must be produced. If you lose track of a child at a beach, you should first enquire at the nearest beach bar or restaurant. In town, a lost child would most likely be taken to the municipal police station or Civil Guard barracks.

I've lost my wallet/handbag.   **He perdido mi cartera/bolso.**

I want to report a theft.   **Quiero denunciar un robo.**

CUSTOMS and ENTRY REQUIREMENTS

Citizens of the UK, Ireland, the US, Canada, Australia and New Zealand require only a valid passport to enter Ibiza. Citizens of South Africa need a visa. If in doubt, check with a travel agent before departure. You are usually entitled to stay in Spain for up to 90 days. If you expect to remain longer, a Spanish consulate or tourist office can advise you.

The severely uniformed, white-gloved Spanish customs officials may ask you to open your suitcase for inspection. If you are stopped for any reason, honesty and courtesy should help move procedures along quickly.

Duty and exemptions. As Spain is part of the EU, free exchange of goods for personal use is permitted between Ibiza and the UK and Ireland. Duty-free sales have now been discontinued for EU citizens. For residents of non-EU countries, restrictions are as follows.

Australia: 250 cigarettes or 250 g tobacco; 1 litre alcohol; Canada: 200 cigarettes and 50 cigars and 400 g tobacco; 1.14 litres spirits or wine or 8.5 litres beer; New Zealand: 200 cigarettes or 50 cigars or 250 g tobacco; 4.5 litres wine or beer and 1.1 litres spirits; South Africa: 400 cigarettes and 50 cigars and 250 g tobacco; 2 litres wine and 1 litre spirits; US: 200 cigarettes and 100 cigars or a 'reasonable amount' of tobacco.

Currency restrictions. Visitors may bring an unlimited amount of Spanish or foreign currency into the country. On departure, however, you must declare any amount beyond the equivalent of €30,000. If you plan to carry large sums in and out again, it's wise to declare your currency on arrival as well as on departure.

I've nothing to declare.	**No tengo nada que declarar.**
It's for my personal use.	**Es para mi uso personal.**

D

DRIVING
To take a car into Spain, citizens of EU member countries do not need an International Driving Permit (other visitors should check with their automobile association), but because it includes text in Spanish it can be useful in case of difficulties with the police. You are only legally required to have your national driving licence. You must also carry your vehicle's registration papers as well as a Green Card or other document extending your regular insurance policy, making it valid in foreign countries. With the latter insurance document, available from your automobile association or insurance company, you will also get a bail bond. However, few visitors take a car to Ibiza and most of the following applies to drivers of hired cars.

Ibiza and Formentera

Driving conditions. The rules on the islands are the same as in mainland Spain and the rest of the continent: drive on the right, overtake on the left, yield right of way to vehicles coming from the right. Spanish drivers tend to use their horn when overtaking. Use of seat belts is obligatory; fines for non-compliance are high.

The roads on Ibiza are still a few years behind the times but are improving. There are a few good main thoroughfares, especially that between Eivissa and Sant Antoni, and from the airport to the capital, and the road to Sant Josep is undergoing renovations that should be finished by the summer season of 2004. Most of the minor roads, however, are narrow and twisting, often filled with potholes and badly signposted. Horse-drawn carts, donkeys, sheep and goats can become perils on the road if you come upon them unexpectedly. When passing through villages, drive with extra care, and give plenty of leeway to motorcycles, scooters and bicycles.

Speed limits. 100 km/h (62 mph) on main roads, 90 km/h (56 mph) on minor roads and 50 km/h (32 mph) in built-up areas. The speed limit for cars towing trailers or caravans is 80 km/h (50 mph).

Traffic violations. The armed Civil Guard *(Guardia Civil)* patrol the few highways of Ibiza in cars or on motorcycles. Always in pairs, they look tough but are actually very courteous and will stop to help anyone in trouble. They're also severe on lawbreakers. If you receive a fine, you will be expected to pay it on the spot. The most common offences include overtaking without indicators flashing, travelling too close to the car in front and travelling with a burned-out headlight or rear light. (Spanish law requires you to carry a spare bulb at all times.)

Parking. In Eivissa, Sant Antoni and Santa Eulària, the traffic police have become much stricter about parking; cars are either towed to the police pound (behind Avinguda Isidoro Macabich) or clamped. Getting the clamp *(cepo)* removed can be a time-consuming and expensive process.

Fuel and oil. Most service stations are open Monday to Saturday from about 7am to 10pm, but a few of the larger, self-service stations are open 24 hours (the *Diario de Ibiza* carries a list of those that remain open on Sunday and fiestas). In rual areas, petrol stations are few and far between. As in the rest of the EU, cars all run on lead-free or lead-replacement petrol, or diesel. Fuel is slightly cheaper than in the UK but will seem expensive to US visitors.

Breakdowns. Because of the heavy workload and a shortage of qualified mechanics, repairs can take longer than at home. Spare parts are readily available for Spanish-built cars, and for some of the better-known European makes, but parts for others might be difficult to obtain. Most of the bigger car hire firms provide a rescue service as part of the contract. In emergencies, tel: 062 *(Guardia Civil)*.

Road signs. Most road signs are the standard pictographs used throughout Europe. However, the following may be useful:

Aparcamiento	Parking
Atención	Caution
Baches	Potholes
Blandones	Soft shoulders
Bordes deteriorados	Deteriorated road edges
Ceda el paso	Give way
Despacio	Slow
Desviación	Diversion
Escuela	School

Estacionamiento prohibido/ Prohibido aparcar	No parking
Obras	Road construction
¡Pare!	Stop
Peatones	Pedestrians
Peligro	Danger
Puesto de socorro	First-aid post
Salida de camiones	Truck exit
(International) driving licence	**carné de conducir (internacional)**
car registration papers	**permiso de circulación**
Green Card	**Carta Verde**
Are we on the right road for … ?	**¿Es ésta la carretera hacia … ?**
Fill the tank, please, with premium.	**Llénelo, por favor, con super.**

Fluid measures

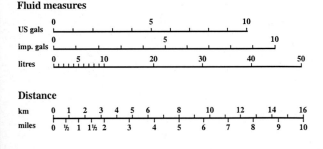

Distance

Check the oil/tyres/battery.	**Por favor, controle el aceite/los neumáticos/la batería.**
I've had a breakdown.	**Mi coche se ha estropeado.**
There's been an accident.	**Ha habido un accidente.**

E

ELECTRICITY *(corriente eléctrica)*

Supplies on the islands are mostly 220-volt AC, at least in the areas where most visitors stay; in rural areas some may still be 125-volts. To play safe, ask at your hotel desk. Sockets are the round two-pin type, so adapters are usually necessary and can be bought before you go, in UK stores or at the airport. Occasionally, especially when it rains, there is a brief blackout. Most hotels supply a candle in every room.

What's the voltage?	**¿Cuál es el voltaje?**
125 or 220?	**¿ciento veinticinco (125) o doscientos veinte (220)?**
an adapter	**un adaptador**
a battery	**una pila**

EMBASSIES and CONSULATES *(embajadas; consulados)*

Almost all Western European countries have consular offices on Ibiza and Majorca, or in Barcelona. All embassies are located in Madrid. If you run into trouble with the authorities or the police, consult your consulate for advice.

Australian consulate:	Gran Via Carles III 98, Barcelona; tel: 933 309 496.
Canadian consulate:	Edificio Goya, Calle Núñez de Balboa 35, 28001 Madrid; tel: 914 233 250.

Irish consulate: Carrer San Miquel 68, 8ª, Palma de Mallorca; tel: 971 719 244.

New Zealand consulate: Traveseria de Gràcia 64, Barcelona; tel: 932 090 399.

UK vice-consulate: Avinguda Isidoro Macabich 45, Eivissa; tel: 971 301 818.

US consulate: Edificio Reina Constanza, Passeig Marítim (Porto Pi), 8, 9-D, Palma de Mallorca; tel: 971 403 707/ 971 403 905.

Where's the British/ American consulate?	**¿Dónde está el consulado británico/americano?**
It's very urgent.	**Es muy urgente.**
I need to make an urgent telephone call.	**Necesito hacer una llamada urgente.**

EMERGENCIES *(urgencias)*
The following emergency telephone numbers are common to all the Balearic Islands:

General emergency number: **112**

Police: **091**

Ambulance: **061**

G

GAY and LESBIAN TRAVELLERS
Ibiza is a popular place with gay and lesbian travellers. This is truly a place to relax and have fun. The island has a host of bars, clubs, cafés, restaurants and hotels and holiday apartments aimed specifically at gay tourists. Contact Ben Amics, the Gay and Lesbian Association of the Balearics, Apartado de Correos 469,

Carrer Conquistador 2, Palma de Mallorca, tel: 971 723 058, toll-free 900 777 500, Mon–Fri 7–9pm, e-mail: benamics@benamics.com, <www.benamics.com>. Another useful web site is <www.gayinspain.com/baleares>.

GETTING THERE

There are numerous ways of getting to the island and a complex range of fares and regulations that can be quite confusing. You can find plenty of information on the Internet, or in the travel sections of Sunday newspapers, but a reliable travel agent who knows the latest fares and special deals can be invaluable.

From the UK:

By air. GB Airways offer direct flights to Ibiza from the UK from May to October; some BA and Iberia flights may also go direct, but most necessitate a connecting flight in Madrid, Barcelona or Palma de Mallorca. In winter, there are currently no direct flights. Charter flights nearly always go direct to Ibiza, and usually have seats available for independent travellers. Budget airlines worth checking out for flights in summer are <www.easyjet.com>, from London Luton; <www.britannia direct.com>, from all major UK airports; <www.bmibaby.com>, from East Midlands; and <www.flybe.com>, from Southampton.

Charter flights and package tours (including flight, transfers, hotel and meals, usually half-board) are the most popular and inexpensive ways of visiting Ibiza. UK travel agents should always offer guarantees in case of bankruptcy or cancellation by the hotels or airlines. The majority also insist on insurance and if you don't have personal insurance, they will arrange it for you.

Fly-drive packages, which include the use of a car on Ibiza, are also available.

By car ferry, hovercraft or Eurotunnel. These methods of travel would only be used by people who plan to spend some time travelling in Spain as well as visiting the Balearic Islands. They are time-consuming and costly compared with flying to the islands and hiring a car when you get there. During the summer, when ferry space for the Channel crossing is at a premium, be sure you have a reservation (<www.seafrance.com> or <www.poferries.com>). The hovercraft from Dover to Calais takes 35–45 minutes and costs only a little more than the ferry (<www.hoverspeed.co.uk>). The Eurotunnel crossing from Folkestone to Calais also takes about 35 minutes (tel: 08705 35 35 35, <ww.eurotunnel.com>). The route from Paris is entirely via toll motorway to Barcelona or Valencia, from where you can get a ferry *(see below)*.

By sea. Car ferries run from Barcelona, Valencia and Palma de Mallorca to Ibiza; contact Trasmediterránea, tel: 902 454 645, <www.trasmediterranea.com> or Baleària, tel: 902 160 180, <www.balearia.net>. The latter company is inaugurating a new, twice-weekly, super-fast ferry in January 2004 (journey time 3hours 40 minutes). During the summer months Baleària also runs a car-ferry service between Denia and Sant Antoni and between Denia and Formentera. From 2004, Trasmediterránea will also operate between Sant Antoni and Denia. Reservations for vehicle space can be difficult to obtain in the high season and are quite expensive. There are frequent ferries and hydrofoils from Ibiza to La Savina, Formentera *(see page 118)*.

From North America:

By air. Direct daily flights to Madrid, and frequent flights to Barcelona, with connections to Ibiza, operate from Miami, New York and Montreal. Or you can fly to London and get a connecting flight from there. Discounted plans include APEX and

Excursion fares. Charter flights and package tours are available through airlines as well as travel agents, and you'll also find charter flights organised by private organisations and companies. Check <www.adventure-bound.com> or <www.priceline.com> for good deals from New York. The ITX (Inclusive Tour Excursion) lets you book only seven days ahead for a seven- to 45-day stay. You can pay to extend your stay by up to another 45 days. There's an added fee if you plan additional stops along the way.

GUIDES and INTERPRETERS *(guías; intérpretes)*
Local tourist offices can direct you to qualified guides and interpreters and will also inform you of the general price range. In most centres, an English-speaking guide can be hired at short notice.

We'd like an English-speaking guide.	**Queremos un guía que hable inglés.**
I need an English interpreter.	**Necesito un intérprete de inglés.**

H

HEALTH and MEDICAL CARE
The most common cause of illness among tourists on Ibiza is an excess of sun, food or alcohol – or a combination of all three. The motto to remember is everything in moderation. Wear sunglasses and a hat and protect your skin by using lots of high-factor sunscreen. Drink plenty of water, as it's easy to get dehydrated in the heat, and it's safest to stick to bottled water. Note that practically no Ibiza beaches maintain a lifeguard.

Insurance. Make certain your health insurance policy covers illness or accident while on holiday, including repatriation if necessary. Before leaving home, British citizens should apply at any main post office for form E111, which covers a reciprocal health care agreement between the UK and EU countries. However, it does not cover all the medical assistance you might need; and you usually have to pay at the point of delivery and reclaim the money later.

Doctors and hospitals. There are doctors in the towns on Ibiza and their consulting hours are posted outside their surgeries. For less serious matters, first-aid personnel *(practicantes)* can be consulted. Some *practicantes* make daily rounds of the major tourist hotels. There are a number of outpatient clinics on the island, and one of them operates round the clock in Eivissa. In the event of emergency, your hotel staff will probably send you there.

Pharmacies/drugstores *(farmacias)*. Pharmacies are usually open during shopping hours. After hours, one pharmacy in each town is always on duty for emergencies. Its address is posted daily in the windows of the other outlets.

a dentist	**un dentista**
a doctor	**un médico**
an ambulance	**una ambulancia**
hospital	**hospital**
an upset stomach	**molestias de estómago**
sunstroke	**insolación**
Get a doctor quickly!	**¡Llamen a un médico rápidamente!**

HOLIDAYS

The following holidays are the national holidays of Spain. There are so many religious, civic or minor holidays celebrated on Ibiza that they seem to come every two weeks. Banks and most shops will close for the day. You might be able to help celebrate one of the more colourful local occasions. Since nearly every town is named after a saint, the saints' days take the form of local fiestas in the respective places. Eivissa lacks a saint's name but not a patron. On 5 August each year, the residents celebrate the feast day of Our Lady of the Snows. *(See pages 73–4 for details of fiestas in different parts of Ibiza and Formentera.)*

1 January	*Año Nuevo*	New Year's Day
6 January	*Epifanía*	Epiphany
19 March	*San José*	St Joseph's Day
1 May	*Día del Trabajo*	Labour Day
25 July	*Día del Santiago Apóstol*	St James's Day
15 August	*Asunción*	Assumption
12 October	*Día de la Hispanidad*	Discovery of America Day
1 November	*Todos los Santos*	All Saints' Day
6 December	*Día de la Constitución Española*	Constitution Day
25 December	*Navidad*	Christmas Day

Movable dates:

Jueves Santo	Maundy Thursday
Viernes Santo	Good Friday
Lunes de Pascua	Easter Monday
Corpus Christi	Corpus Christi
Inmaculada Concepción	Immaculate Conception

LANGUAGE

Castilian, the national language of Spain, is understood everywhere. However, the islanders customarily speak Ibicenco, a variant of Catalan. Since Castilian is not the first language for all

Ibiza and Formentera

Ibizan residents, they may speak it more slowly than mainland Spaniards do. Rudimentary English, German and French are generally spoken in tourist areas. On a brief visit to Ibiza it would be difficult to learn a lot of the local language, although a few words will go a long way and always be appreciated. If you speak any Spanish there will be no problem making yourself understood. If not, you will still get by.

Ibicenco	*English*	*Castilian*
Bon dia	Good morning	**Buenos días**
Bones tardes	Good afternoon	**Buenas tardes**
Bona nit	Good night	**Buenas noches**
Gràcies	Thank you	**Gracias**
De res	You're welcome	**De nada**
Per favor	Please	**Por favor**
Adéu	Goodbye	**Adiós**

NUMBERS

0	cero	12	doce	31	treinta y uno
1	uno	13	trece	32	treinta y dos
2	dos	14	catorce	40	cuarenta
3	tres	15	quince	50	cincuenta
4	cuatro	16	dieciséis	60	sesenta
5	cinco	17	diecisiete	70	setenta
6	seis	18	dieciocho	80	ochenta
7	siete	19	diecinueve	90	noventa
8	ocho	20	veinte	100	cien
9	nueve	21	veintiuno	101	ciento uno
10	diez	22	veintidós	500	quinientos
11	once	30	treinta	1,000	mil

The *Berlitz Spanish Phrase Book and Dictionary* covers most situations you're likely to encounter in your travels in Spain. In addition, the *Berlitz Spanish–English/English–Spanish Pocket Dictionary* contains a 12,500-word glossary of each language, plus a menu-reader supplement.

SOME USEFUL EXPRESSIONS

where/when/how	**dónde/cuándo/cómo**
how long/how far	**cuànto tiempo/a qué distancia**
yesterday/today/tomorrow	**ayer/hoy/mañana**
day/week/month/year	**día/semana/mes/año**
left/right	**izquierda/derecha**
up/down	**arriba/bajo**
good/bad	**bueno/malo**
big/small	**grande/pequeño**
cheap/expensive	**barato/caro**
hot/cold	**caliente/frío**
old/new	**viejo/nuevo**
open/closed	**abierto/cerrado**
here/there	**aquí/allí**
free (vacant)/occupied	**libre/ocupado**
early/late	**temprano/tarde**
easy/difficult	**fácil/difícil**
What does this mean?	**¿Qué quiere decir esto?**
Please write it down.	**Por favor, escríbalo.**
Is there an admission charge?	**¿Se debe pagar la entrada?**
I'd like …	**Quisiera …**
Have you something less expensive?	**¿Tiene algo más barato?**

Ibiza and Formentera

Just a minute.	**Un momento.**
Get a doctor quickly!	**¡Llamen a un médico ràpidamente!**
I'd like film for this camera.	**Quisiera un carrete para esta máquina.**
How long will it take to develop (and print) this film?	**¿Cuánto tardará en revelar (y sacar copias de) este carrete?**
May I take a picture?	**¿Puedo sacar una fotografía?**

LAUNDRY and DRY CLEANING

Most hotels will handle laundry and dry cleaning, but they usually charge more than will a public laundry *(lavandería)* or a dry cleaner *(tintorería)*. You'll find do-it-yourself launderettes in a few areas.

I must have this for tomorrow morning.	**Lo necesito para mañana por la mañana.**

M

MAPS

Some places are known by both their Castilian and Catalan names, although Catalan is more generally used. To add to the confusion, maps aren't always consistent in their use of place names, so you may see a beach referred to as both a *playa* (Castilian) and a *platja* (Catalan), while a street may be either a *calle* or a *carrer*. Maps obtainable from tourist offices should be sufficient for your needs, but if you want something more detailed go to a *librería* (bookshop).

a street plan of...	**un plano de la ciudad de …**
a road map of the island	**un mapa de carreteras de la isla**

MEDIA

Newspapers and magazines *(periódico; revista)*. During the height of the tourist season, all major British and continental European newspapers are on sale in Ibiza on the day of their publication or the following morning. European and US magazines are always available, as is the Paris-based *International Herald Tribune*. For additional news, the local *Ibiza News,* aimed at English-speaking tourists, is published weekly.

If you can read a bit of Spanish, you might also be interested in the daily *Diario de Ibiza,* the local daily, or the Ibiza edition of *Última Hora*. There is also a useful on-line English newspaper, the *Ibiza Sun*, that appears every Wednesday throughout the year; go to <www.theibizasun.net>.

Do you have any English-language newspapers? **¿Tienen periódicos en inglés?**

Radio and television. Most hotels have television in the rooms, or television lounges, but programmes are usually broadcast in Spanish. In resorts like Sant Antoni, with a large proportion of English visitors, bars have English satellite TV stations broadcasting sports events. Ibiza's local commercial radio stations have programmes in English and German, at least during the summer season, and one station also broadcasts in French and Italian. The BBC and Voice of America are available to travellers with short-wave radios.

MONEY MATTERS

Spain's monetary unit is the euro (abbreviated €), which is divided into 100 cents. Bank notes are available in denominations of 500, 200, 100, 50, 20, 10 and 5 euros. There are coins for 2 and 1 euro, and for 50, 20, 10, 5, 2 and 1 cent.

Exchange offices. Outside normal banking hours (see OPENING HOURS), many travel agencies and other businesses displaying a *cambio* sign will change foreign currency into euros. The exchange rate is a bit less favourable than in the banks. Both banks and exchange offices pay slightly more for traveller's cheques than for cash. Always take your passport with you for identification when you change money.

Credit cards. All the internationally recognised cards are accepted by hotels, most restaurants and businesses in Spain.

ATMs. Cash machines are now ubiquitous in Spain, but on the islands you'll find them only in cities and tourist resorts. They dispense currency in various euro denominations. Using an ATM with your credit or debit card is by far the most convenient and cheapest way of obtaining euros.

Traveller's cheques. Shops, banks, hotels and travel agencies in tourist areas accept traveller's cheques, but you're likely to get a better exchange rate at a national or regional bank. Remember to carry your passport if you expect to cash a traveller's cheque.

Paying with cash. Although many larger shops and bars will accept payment in sterling or dollars, you're better off paying in euros. Shops will invariably give you less than the bank rate for foreign currency.

Where's the nearest bank/ currency exchange office?	**¿Dónde está el banco/la oficina de cambio más cercana?**
I want to change some pounds/dollars.	**Quiero cambiar unas libras/ unos dólares.**
Do you accept traveller's cheques?	**¿Acepta usted checks de viajero?**
Can I pay with this credit card?	**¿Puedo pagar con esta tarjeta de crédito?**

O

OPENING HOURS

Schedules on Ibiza revolve around the siesta, one of the really great Spanish institutions. Most shops are open from 9am to 1pm and then from 4pm to 8pm; offices keep similar hours, but usually close at 7pm. In the main tourist resorts, shops may stay open all day in summer and close later at night, as do large supermarkets. Banks generally open from 8.30am to 1.30pm, Monday to Friday, and till 12.30pm on Saturday. Post offices open from 9am to 2pm, Monday to Friday, and till noon on Saturday. The main post office in Eivissa keeps longer hours: 9am to 1.30pm and 3pm to 8pm. Most churches are open from 8am to noon, and 5pm till 8pm

Restaurants start serving lunch about 1pm and dinner (earlier here than on the mainland) is generally between 8pm and 11pm.

P

POLICE *(policía)*

Dial **091** for emergency police assistance.

There are three police forces in Spain. The best known is the *Guardia Civil* (Civil Guard). Each sizeable town also has its *Policía Municipal* (Municipal Police), wearing navy blue uniforms with blue shirts. Members of the third unit, the *Cuerpo Nacional de Policía* (National Police) – a national anti-crime unit – wear a navy blue uniform with white shirts. You can call on any one of the three forces (all armed) if you need police assistance. Spanish police are efficient, strict, and courteous to foreign visitors.

Where's the nearest police station?	**¿Dónde està la comisaría màs cercana?**

POST OFFICES

Post offices *(correos)* are used for mail, telex and telegrams only. You cannot make telephone calls from them. Some post offices limit acceptance of registered mail to certain times. They often stay open a few hours after the normal closing for telegraph business. Mailboxes are yellow with red stripes.

Parcels *(paquetes)* up to 2kg (4.4lbs) can be mailed from local post offices. Heavier parcels must be sent from the main post office in Eivissa *(see below)*.

If you don't know in advance where you'll be staying, you can have your mail addressed to *lista de correos* (Poste Restante or General Delivery) at whichever town is most convenient. You must take your passport with you to the post office for identification when you collect your mail.

The main post office in Ibiza is at Carrer Madrid 21, Eivissa, tel: 971 311 380) In Formentera, the man office is at Plaça Constitució, Sant Fransesc, tel: 971 322 243.

Have you received any mail for me?	**¿Ha recibido correo para mí?**
A stamp for this letter/postcard, please.	**Por favor, un sello para esta carta/tarjeta postal.**
express (special delivery)	**urgente**
airmail	**vía aérea**
registered	**certificado**

PUBLIC TRANSPORT

Bus services. On Ibiza the bus service hasn't quite caught up with the tourist boom, but it is cheap and reliable. There is a half-hourly service in summer between Eivissa and Sant Antoni, Santa Eulària and Portinatx. Private bus services also operate local runs to beaches. Check timetables and be careful not to miss the last bus. Eivissa has its own urban bus service which also runs out to the suburbs and to the nearby beaches. Note that there's no east–west bus service across the island. To get from Sant Antoni to Santa Eulària, you must change in Eivissa, a jaunt which takes about 90 minutes, while a direct journey would take a quarter of that time. In summer a Discobus service operates between the major resorts from midnight to 6.30am.

On Formentera the bus service is irregular and subject to seasonal change; on the whole it is best not to rely on it.

When is the next bus to…?	**¿Cuándo sale el próximo autobús para … ?**
one-way (single)	**ida**
round-trip (return)	**ida y vuelta**

Taxis. The letters *SP* on the front and rear bumpers of a car don't stand for Spain; they mean *servicio público,* and the car is a taxi. It might also have a green light in the front window and a taxi sign. Whatever it looks like, it's a reasonably economical mode of transport. Some Ibiza taxis have meters but drivers don't always use them, so agree on a price before setting out. The major towns have taxi ranks where the taxis, not the customers, have to line up most of the time; fixed fares should be displayed on a notice board at these ranks.

What's the fare to …	**¿Cuánto es la tarifa a … ?**

Boat services. Ferries link Ibiza with mainland Spain (see GETTING THERE). Getting to Formentera from Ibiza is quick and easy: the trip to the port of La Savina from Ibiza takes just over one hour by ferry and 25 minutes by Linea Jet hydrofoil. The journey can be rough and in adverse conditions the hydrofoils are cancelled. Both ferry and hydrofoil services are frequent during high season (10 sailings a day) but reduced at other times. Contact Trasmapi, tel: 971 314 005, e-mail: trasmapi@insotel.com. There are also hydrofoil services to Majorca (a two-hour trip) as well as numerous boat excursions around Ibiza itself. The frequency of services increases considerably during the high season (1 July–30 September).

RELIGION

The national religion of Spain is Roman Catholicism. On Ibiza, mass is said in no fewer than 33 different Catholic churches. In summer, notices of masses in foreign languages are posted outside major churches in Sant Antoni and Santa Eulària. Protestant services are also held. Look for notices on hotel bulletin boards. There is no Jewish congregation on Ibiza. When visiting churches as a tourist, dress modestly and respect the privacy of those who are there to pray.

What time is mass/ the service?	**¿A qué hora es la misa/ el servicio?**
Is it in English?	**¿Es en inglés?**

TELEPHONE (teléfono)

The international code for Spain is **34** with **9** preceding each area code. For the Balearics, the area code is **971**. This must be dialled even within the islands and towns themselves. To reach a number in the islands from the UK, dial 00 34 + 971 + the six-digit local telephone number.

To reach other areas of Spain from Ibiza, dial **9** then the appropriate area code (Madrid is 1; Barcelona is 3; Valencia is 6), followed by the local number.

Although Ibiza's automatic dialling system allows you to dial numbers throughout Spain, it may sometimes be impossible to reach a number across town.

Overseas calls can be made from your hotel (the most expensive way), but you can also make calls at public telephone offices called *locutorios*. This is much quieter than making a call on the street, and more convenient, as an attendant will place the call for you, and you pay afterwards. For most calls, including international calls, at pay phones, it's wise to use a phone card *(tarjeta telefónica)*, which can be purchased at any *estanco* (tobacconist's shop; look for the sign *'Tabacs'*).

If you don't have a phone card, be sure to have enough change to complete your call, as these public phones have no numbers and the other party cannot ring you back. For international direct dialling, wait for the dial tone, then dial 00, then the country code, area or city code (omitting the initial zero) and local number. There are instructions in English and other languages in the phone booths.

To reverse the charges, ask for *'Cobro revertido'*. For a person-to-person call, specify *'Persona a persona'*.

E-mail. There is an increasing number of e-mail cafés in Eivissa and the resorts, which mostly charge by the half-hour or hour. All rates are pretty similar. Otherwise, your laptop will need a Spanish modem-adapter plug to link up to the local telephone.

Fax. Most hotels have fax facilities. Be sure to get written proof that the fax has been sent and received.

Can you get me this number in …?	**¿Puede communicarme con este número en …?**

TIME ZONES

Ibiza is on Spanish time, which is the same as in most of Western Europe: Greenwich Mean Time + one hour. In summer, clocks are put one hour ahead (GMT + 2). The following chart shows times in winter:

Ibiza and Formentera

New York	London	**Ibiza**	Sydney	Auckland
6am	11am	**noon**	10pm	midnight

What time is it?   **¿Qué hora es?**

TIPPING

A service charge is normally included in your restaurant bill (look for the words *servicio incluido*). If not, a tip of 10 percent is usual. It is also appropriate to tip porters, service-station attendants, taxi drivers, hairdressers and others for their service. The following chart gives some suggestions:

Hotel porter (per bag)	minimum 50 cents
Hotel maid (at end of week)	5 euros
Waiter	5–10 percent
Taxi driver	10 percent
Hairdresser/barber	10 percent
Tour guide	10 percent

TOILETS *(servicios)*

There are many expressions for toilets in Spanish: *aseos, servicios, WC* and *retretes*. The first two are the most common. Toilet doors usually have a 'C' for *Caballeros* (gentlemen), and an 'S' for *Señoras* (ladies).

Public conveniences on Ibiza are pretty rare, but just about every bar and restaurant has a toilet that can be used by the public. It is considered polite to buy a cup of coffee or a glass of wine if you drop in specifically to use the toilets, but many places either don't mind or don't notice. If they object to non-customers using the facilities, they usually keep the key behind the bar so that you have to ask for it.

Where are the toilets?   **¿Dónde estàn los servicios?**

TOURIST INFORMATION *(información turística)*
Spanish National Tourist Offices abroad:
Australia: International House, Suite 44, 104 Bathurst Street, PO Box A-675, 2000 Sydney NSW, tel: 02-264 7966.
Canada: 2 Bloor Street West, Suite 3402, Toronto, Ontario M4W 3E2; tel: 1416-961 3131, e-mail: toronto@tourspain.es.
UK: 22–23 Manchester Square, London W1U 3PX, tel: 020 7486 8077; brochure line, tel: 09063 640 630, email: info.londres@tourspain.es; <www.tourspain.co.uk>.
US: Water Tower Place, Suite 915 East, 845 North Michigan Avenue, Chicago, IL 60611, tel: 312-944 0216/642 1992.
8383 Wilshire Boulevard, Suite 960, 90211 Beverly Hills, CA 90211, tel: 213-658 7188.
666 5th Avenue, 35th floor, New York, NY 10103, tel: 212-265 8822, fax: 212 265 8864, email: oetny@tourspain.es.
1221 Brickell Avenue, Miami, FL 33131, tel: 305-358 1992.

Tourist Offices in Ibiza and Formentera:
Oficina de Turismo, Passeig Vara de Rey 13, Eivissa, tel: 971 301 900, fax: 971 301 562, e-mail: IB.Mintour05@bitel.es.
Oficina de Turismo, Paseo de Ses Fonts, s/n, Sant Antoni de Portmany, tel: 971343363, fax: 971344175, e-mail: IB.Mintour03@bitel.es.
Oficina de Turismo, Mariano Riquer Wallis, s/n, Santa Eulària des Riu, tel: 971 330 728, fax: 971 332 959, e-mail: IB.Mintour02@bitel.es.
Oficina de Turismo, Llevant 7 (Sant Llorenç), S'Illot, tel/fax: 971 810 699, e-mail: MA.Mintour06@bitel.es.
Oficina de Turismo, Port de la Savina, Formentera, tel: 971 325 057, fax: 971 322 825.

Where's the tourist office?   **¿Dónde està la oficina de turismo?**

TRAVELLERS WITH DISABILITIES

Many modern hotels have wheelchair access and facilities for travellers with disabilities, but not all tourist sites and attractions are accessible. For more general information, consult the online magazine Disability View, Craven Publishing 15–39 Durham Street, Kinning Park, Glasgow GW1 1BS, tel: 0141 419 0044, fax: 0141 419 0077, <www.disabilityview.co.uk>, e-mail: info@disabilityview.co.uk.

WEBSITES

You can learn a lot about Ibiza and Formentera on the Internet. Check out the commercial sites at <www.ibiza-online.com>, <www.ibiza-spotlight.com>, <www.theibizasun.net> and <www.ibiza-info.com>. Official sites of the Balearic government you may find useful are <www.baleares.com> and <www.visitbalears.com>. Search engines such as Google, Excite and Yahoo! will find additional travel-oriented sites if you just enter the word Ibiza.

Recommended Hotels

This selection lists hotels in and around the major resorts (Eivissa, Sant Antoni and Santa Eulària), plus a few addresses in the areas of Sant Miquel and Sant Josep. We then list accommodation on the island of Formentera.

The Spanish tourism authorities allot stars to hotels according to criteria that do not always correspond to price or even to degree of comfort. The island's hotels have three basic categories: *casas de huéspedes* (guesthouses, also known as *pensións* or *fondas*); *hostals* (family hotels, officially allotted one, two or three stars); and higher-class hotels (ranging officially from two to five stars).

In some establishments, not all rooms will have an en suite bathroom. Make sure you check this when making your reservation. Rates for rooms with shared bathrooms will be lower.

Your nightly room charge will usually, but not always, include breakfast; again, check when making the booking. Some hotels quote rates for half-board accommodation (i.e. with the evening meal included).

Details of hotels with access and facilities for people with disabilities are available from RADAR, 12 City Forum, 250 City Road, London, EC1V 8AF; tel: 020-7250 3222.

The price categories in the following list represent the average high-season daily rate for a double room with bath; a value-added tax (IVA) of 7 percent is extra. However, rates vary greatly so these are given only as an indication. The more modest hotels and pensions may not accept credit cards, but the vast majority do.

€€€	above 120 euros
€€	60–120 euros
€	below 60 euros

Eivissa (Ibiza Town)

Algarb €€ *Platja d'en Bossa; tel: 971 301 716; fax: 971 301 904.* Mammoth modern hotel right on beach, 3km (2 miles) from the centre of Eivissa. 408 rooms.

Cenit €€ *Archiduque Luis Salvador s/n; tel: 971 301 404.* Big, nicely kept hotel in Puig des Molins quarter near Figueretas beach. Beautiful harbour view from terrace. 62 rooms.

El Corsario €€ *Poniente 5, Dalt Vila; tel: 971 393 212; fax: 971 391 953.* Tastefully transformed house, popular with artists and writers since the 1960s, with Ibicenco décor, antique fittings and a grand terrace view over the old town and port. 14 rooms.

El Corso €€ *Platja Talamanca; tel: 971 312 312.* A traditional style hotel, completely refurbished in 1997, close to an excellent beach but only 3km (2 miles) from town, with ferry and bus connections. 58 rooms.

Don Quijote € *Pais Basc 10; tel: 971 301 869; fax: 971 341 358.* A large, high-rise, budget-price hotel near Figueretas beach within walking disance of the town centre. Minimum 7-night stay in high season. 106 rooms.

Mare Nostrum € *Av. Pedro Matutes Noguera; tel: 971 302 662.* Huge, good-value, budget-price beach hotel. All amenities: parking, playground, nursery, hairdressing salon, shops, garden, convention hall, tennis, squash, miniature golf and pool. 528 rooms.

La Marina € *Andenes del Puerto 4; tel: 971 310 172.* Older waterfront building renovated in 1991; not quiet but with great views of boats coming in and out of the port. 25 rooms.

Los Molinos €€€ *Ramón Muntaner 60; tel: 971 302 250; fax: 971 302 504.* Very comfortable hotel in convenient location not far from Figueretas beach, with pleasant garden, terrace and pool overlooking the sea. 147 rooms.

Montesol € *Vara de Rey 2; tel: 971 310 161; fax: 971 310 162.* Popular spot recently renovated in the heart of the Sa Penya harbour quarter, close to Dalt Vila and a one-minute walk from the port. 55 rooms.

Ocean Drive €€€ *Platja de Talamanca 223; tel: 971 318 112; fax: 971 312 228.* Sophisticated, modern design and furnishings. On the yacht harbour with view of Dalt Vila; a short walk from major night clubs. Fine seafood restaurant. 42 rooms.

El Palacio €€€ *Conquista 2; tel: 971 301 478; fax: 971 391 581.* Flashy Swiss-operated hotel in an old, renovated Dalt Vila mansion, with cinematic theme (seven suites and rooms with movie-star names and décor) and a private car park (a rarity in the old-town district).

Parque € *Vicente Cuervo 3; tel: 971 301 358.* Modest but clean, and centrally located on corner of Vara de Rey. 29 rooms.

Ripoll € *Vicente Cuervo 14; tel: 971 314 275.* Small boarding house with friendly atmosphere. Also apartments. 15 rooms.

Sol y Brisa € *Bartolomé Vicenç Ramón 15; tel: 971 310 818.* Modest but immaculate and bright little boarding house, two minutes from the harbour. 20 rooms.

Torre del Mar €€€ *Platja d'en Bossa; tel: 971 303 050; fax: 971 304 060.* A luxurious hotel on the beach just 1km (½ mile) from the town centre, set in beautiful gardens, with indoor and outdoor pools, a sauna, and a highly recommended restaurant. 217 rooms.

Tres Carabelas €€ *Platja d'en Bossa; tel: 971 302 416.* Popular hotel in scenic location at beach, offering all modern conveniences including pool, tennis courts, gym, sauna, miniature golf and garden terrace. 245 rooms.

La Ventana €€€ *Sa Carrossa 13; tel: 971 390 857; fax: 971 390 145.* Fine value and comfort on picturesque little square in old Dalt Vila, with upper rooms and terrace commanding superb view over harbour. Good restaurant. 13 rooms.

Sant Antoni and District

Arenal €€€ *Av. Dr Fleming 16; tel: 971 340 112; fax: 971 342 965.* Well-run, well-equipped modern hotel on the east side of the harbour on a very popular beach, with an easy walk to shops. Spacious rooms, good atmosphere. 131 rooms.

Bergantin €€ *Albacete 5–7, Platja de s'Estanyol; tel: 971 341 461.* Large, modern hotel with attractive seafront location and a good pool. Bus stop right outside. 253 rooms.

Es Plá € *Av. Portmany; tel: 971 341 154; fax: 971 340 452.* Big hotel with modern facilities, without a sea view but located in pleasant grounds 200m (220 yds) from beach and a three-minute walk from the town centre.

Florencio € *Soledad 38; tel: 971 340 723.* This modest but well-kept hotel has cheerful service and a convenient location not far from the town centre. 104 rooms.

Gran Sol €€ *Soledad 49; tel: 971 341 106; fax: 971 341 267.* Large and comfortable modern hotel at the northeast corner of town, not far from the centre. 138 rooms.

March *Portmany 10; tel: 971 340 062.* Delightful, modestly priced family hotel with exceptionally friendly service, close to the centre, with a garden and a pool. 86 rooms.

Milord I €€ *Sant Antoni; tel: 971 340 612; fax: 971 340 966.* For details, see Milord II, below. 153 rooms.

Milord II Fiesta €€ *Sant Antoni; tel: 971 341 227; fax: 971 340 966.* The sister high-rise hotels Milord I and Milord II stand together, across the bay from town. They share fine facilities, including nightly music, two pools and access to several beaches with good water sports. Book well in advance. 218 rooms.

Mitjorn € *Carrer del Far 10; tel: 971 340 902.* Small, friendly, well-kept boarding house close to the port, with view of bay from upper floors, and a pool. Good value. 18 rooms.

Norte € *Barcelona 7; tel: 971 340 127.* Pleasant boarding house in centre of town, a five-minute walk from harbour. Garden and pool. 56 rooms.

Osiris €€ *Carrer Pino 1; tel: 971 340 916.* Comfortable medium-sized hotel, efficiently run in convenient location. 97 rooms.

Palmyra €€€ *Av. Dr Fleming; tel: 971 340 354; fax: 971 312 964.* Handsome, modern hotel with attractive palm-shaded terrace, nicely located on beach about 1km (½ mile) from the centre. First-class water sports and other facilities. 160 rooms.

Ibiza and Formentera

Pike's €€€ *Sa Vorera; tel: 971 342 222; fax: 971 342 312*True luxury in a lovingly renovated 15th-century farmhouse tucked away in beautiful countryside but within easy reach of the sea. Traditional Ibicenco décor in all rooms, swimming pool, tennis, minature golf and VIP card for free access to all major discos. 27 rooms, 22 suites.

San Remo €€ *Port des Torrent, Platja de s'Estanyol; tel: 971 341 150; fax: 971 341 123.* Right on S'Estanyol beach at Sant Antoni Bay, 3km (2 miles) from town centre. Every modern sports facility, nighttime musical entertainment, special facilities for children. 147 rooms.

Tanit €€ *Cala Gràcia; tel: 971 341 300.* Close to the harbour, this is a well run hotel with good facilities. 42 rooms.

Santa Eulària and District

Can Curren Rural Hotel €€€ *Cta Sant Carles Km 12; tel/fax: 971 335 280.* A pleasant rural hotel with attractively furnished rooms, a pool, gym, gardens and stables. 7 rooms.

Cala Nova Playa €€ *Platja Cala Nova; tel: 971 330 300; fax: 971 332 410.* Large, well-run hotel, surrounded by pines, 5km (3 miles) north of Santa Eulària and just 50m/yds from Es Canar beach. Facilities include air conditioning and disco. 305 rooms.

Club Cala Blanca €€€ *Platja es Figueral, San Carlos; tel: 971 335 100; fax: 971 335 040.* **Club Cala Verde** *tel: 971 335 111; fax: 971 335 061.* These twin facilities combine in a large, ultra-modern resort complex with handsome gardens, offering a broad range of water sports and other activities on

Figueral Bay. 320 rooms (Club Cala Blanca); 257 rooms (Club Cala Verde).

Fiesta Don Carlos €€ *Urbanización Siesta; tel: 971 330 128; fax: 971 330 634.* Recently refurbished; set on quiet beach just 1km (½ mile) from town centre, with good water sports facilities and pleasant beach bar. 168 rooms.

La Cala €€ *Sant Jaume 76; tel: 971 330 009; fax: 971 331 512.* Comfortable hotel centrally located by the port and promenade, with garden and swimming pool. 180 rooms.

Las Arenas € *Platja es Canar; tel: 971 330 790.* Overlooking the sea, with simple but clean and comfortable rooms. 20 rooms.

Mayol € *Algemesi 2; tel: 971 330 282.* Modest, functional guesthouse a short walk from beach and marina. 17 rooms.

Mediterraneo € *Pintor Vizcai 1; tel: 971 330 015; fax: 971 339 344.* Bargain-priced family hotel in upper town, with garden, pool and splendid views of bay and countryside. 63 rooms.

Punta Arabí €€ *Punt Arabí (Es Canar); tel: 971 330 152; fax: 971 339 167.* Located close to beaches, with swimming pool and disco. Simply furnished rooms; sea views. Miró style decoration on the façade. 72 rooms and apartments.

Rey € *Sant Josep 17; tel: 971 330 210.* Efficient family boarding house, within easy reach of beach and the town centre's Plaça d'Espanya. 20 rooms.

San Marino €€€ *Ricardo Curtoys Gotarredona 1; tel: 971 330 316; fax: 971 339 076.* Grand, luxuriously appointed modern hotel in heart of town centre but only two minutes from sea. 44 apartment-style rooms.

Ses Estaques € *Platja Ses Estaques; tel: 971 330 200; fax: 971 330 486.* Smart, four-storey hotel popular with package-tour operators but run with a personal touch by a local husband and wife team. 159 rooms.

Sol Los Loros €€€ *Finca Cas Capitá; tel: 971 330 761; fax: 339 542.* High-quality comfort in big seafront hotel with spectacular view over rocky coast, a short walk from town centre. Children's club; tennis; indoor and outdoor pools. 262 rooms.

Tres Torres €€€ *Passeig Marítim s/n, Ses Estaques; tel: 971 330 326; fax: 971 332 085.* Luxurious and recently renovated hotel, near marina and beach; first-rate water sports facilities; tennis; disco. 112 rooms.

Sant Josep

Les Jardins de Palerm €€€ *Afueras s/n; tel: 971 800 318; fax: 971 800 453.* An exclusive haven of tranquillity in taste-fully restored 17th-century country mansion near the village of Sant Josep, south of Sant Antoni Bay. Exquisite gardens. 14 rooms.

Sant Miquel

Club Cartago €€ *Port de Sant Miquel; tel: 971 334 551.* Recommended, smoothly-run hotel in a modernistic building, with steps leading down to a little beach.

Hacienda Na Xamena €€€ *Na Xamena, Sant Miquel; tel: 971 334 500; fax: 971 334 514.* Ibiza's only five-star hotel, stunningly set on a hillside with magnificent views of sea and cliffs. Traditional Ibicenco décor in all rooms. Superb restaurants. 52 rooms, 9 suites.

Formentera

Agua Clara €€ *Cta a Platja de Mitjorn, Ca Mari; tel: 971 328 180; fax: 971 328 229.* Well-kept hotel on sprawling Mitjorn beach on south coast. 25 rooms.

Bellavista €€ *Plaça de la Marina, La Savina; tel: 971 322 236; fax: 971 322 672.* Good guest house with friendly service, a spacious restaurant and harbour-side terrace. 42 rooms.

Cala Saona €€€ *Cala Saona; tel: 971 322 010; fax: 971 322 509.* Well-equipped, modern family hotel, recently expanded, directly overlooking attractive beach on west coast. Swimming pool and tennis courts. 116 rooms.

Casbah Migjorn € *Platja de Mitjorn; tel: 971 322 051; fax: 971 322 595.* Comfortable, pleasant seafront hotel. 29 rooms.

Club Riu La Mola €€€ *Platja de Mitjorn; tel: 971 328 069.* In spectacular setting at the foot of La Mola cliffs. Luxury resort complex, the most expensive on the island, with state-of-the-art water sports, tennis and miniature golf facilities. 328 rooms.

Club Punta Prima €€€ *Venda de Sa Punta, Es Pujols; tel: 971 328 244; fax: 971 328 128.* Newly built on promontory at east end of Es Pujols beach on north coast. Bungalows set in lovely flowering gardens, swimming poool, tennis, children's playground and shopping centre. 94 rooms.

Costa Azul € *Ca Mari, Platja de Mitjorn; tel: 971 328 024; fax: 971 328 994.* A good-quality, low-budget guesthouse at the water's edge. Fine seafood restaurant. 13 rooms.

Fonda Pepe € *Major 68, Sant Ferran; tel: 971 328 033.* An inland village rendezvous popular since the (perhaps legendary) visit of Bob Dylan. Frequented by the hippie crowd, this boarding house has friendly atmosphere, 1960s memorabilia and a good seafood restaurant. 36 rooms.

Formentera Playa €€€ *Platja de Migjorn; tel: 971 328 000; fax: 971 328 035.* One of the bigger and more expensive hotels on Formentera, this four-storey establishment, right on the beach, has all the facilities you would expect of a good quality resort hotel. 357 rooms.

Los Rosales €€ *Es Pujols; tel: 971 328 123; fax: 971 328 161.* Small and functional; close to beach and the centre of town.

Rafalet € *Es Calo; tel/fax: 971 327 016.* Agreeable boarding house, clean and well kept, splendidly situated with restaurant and café terrace on tiny natural harbour. 15 rooms.

Rosamar € *Platja de sa Roqueta, Es Pujols; tel: 971 328 473.* A perfectly adequate little place, near town and beach, good value, with a nice restaurant.

Sa Roqueta € *Platja Es Pujols; tel/fax: 971 328 506.* Beachfront boarding house on small, quiet bay west of La Savina port. Good restaurant. 33 rooms.

Voramar € *Av. Miramar s/n; tel: 971 328 119; fax: 971 328 680.* Small, basic, and friendly *hostal*, housed in an attractive building. 8 rooms.

Recommended Restaurants

The following restaurants are listed by major towns and resort areas. Many establishments are out of town but easily accessible by car or taxi. For out-of-town addresses without street names, we follow the local island convention of naming the highway (for example, Carretera Sant Joan) with – wherever possible – the distance in kilometres measured from the Eivissa starting point.

The list features traditional Ibicenco and Spanish national cuisine but also a few 'international' restaurants specialising in French, Italian and Chinese food. In rare cases where telephone numbers are not given, reservations are not required. However, this is only a selection and half the fun of a holiday is discovering for yourself the countless tapas bars and the ever-changing beach establishments for which telephone reservations are rarely possible.

The following price categories are based on a three-course a la carte meal for one, including house wine.

€€€	over 40 euros
€€	20–40 euros
€	under 20 euros

Eivissa (Ibiza Town)

La Brasa €€ *Pere Sala 3; tel: 971 301 202.* Good seafood and grills served in quiet oasis in busy quarter, with pretty patio and a garden terrace right underneath the ramparts.

Ca N'Alfredo €€ *Vara de Rey 16; tel: 971 311 274.* Eat indoors or on a terrace on the city's handsome esplanade. Robust portions of classical Spanish dishes and fresh seafood.

Casino de Ibiza €€€ *Passeig Joan Carles; tel: 971 313 312.* Excellent but expensive food. Book in advance and take your passport as it's inside the casino.

Celler Balearev €€ *Ignacio Wallis 18; tel: 971 301 031.* On broad avenue running north of Vara de Rey. Ibicenco and Spanish dishes *(paella* a speciality) as well as international cuisine. Traditional wine-cellar complete with old barrels.

El Cigarral €€ *Frare Vicenç Nicolau 9; tel: 971 311 246.* Good beef and especially fine wines – much appreciated by local connoisseurs. On the north side of town.

Dalt Vila €€ *Plaça de la Vila; tel: 971 305 524.* Pleasant terrace for eating out in old-town square. Mediterranean cuisine with Italian specialities.

El Faro €€ *Plaça Garija 4; tel: 971 317 578.* Port-side restaurant with garden terrace. Known for its extremely fresh fish kept in water tank,; outstanding *paella de mariscos* .

Formentera €€ *Plaça de Sa Tertulia; tel: 971 311 024.* Long-established institution, family run for 60 years, in old fisherman's house facing the harbour. Traditional Ibicenco and international cuisine; with *paella* the house speciality.

La Masía d'en Sord € *Carretera Sant Miquel; tel: 971 310 228.* Enchanting 17th-century farmhouse with romantic outdoor terrace and rustic indoor dining room; huge house divided into smaller rooms for greater intimacy. Mediterranean cuisine, with salmon a speciality.

Mesón de Paco €€ *Bartolomé Rosselló 15; tel: 971 314 224.* Attractive, country-style décor, tiled walls, carved wood furnishings. Best of Ibicenco cooking, with a truly robust *paella*.

Nanking € *Bisbe Cardona 8; tel: 971 190 951.* Elegant Cantonese venue, popular with islanders in and out of season.

La Oliva €€ *Santa Cruz 2; tel: 971 305 752.* In the lively quarter of the old town, fine Provençal cuisine is given an Ibicenco touch: grilled seafood, duck with figs in sherry sauce. An annex opposite provides extra seating. Book in high season.

El Olivo €€€ *Plaça de la Vila 8; tel: 971 300 680.* Renowned old-town address with elegant terrace, for sophisticated combination of French and Spanish cuisine. Booking recommended.

El Portalón €€ *Plaça des Desamparats 1–2; tel: 971 303 901.* Right inside ramparts beside main entrance. Fine restaurant with immaculate and friendly service, famous for its seafood salads and *calamares alla plancha y helado* (grilled, cold squid).

S'Anfora €€€ *Bartolomé Rosselló 13; tel: 971 314 226.* Much appreciated by local people for its refined cooking (seafood a speciality) in an elegant setting.

S'Oficina €€€ *Avinguda d'España 6; tel: 971 300 016.* Ibicencos flock here for Basque cuisine on shady terrace in town centre, not far from Vara de Rey. Huge tanks of lobsters and shellfish as well as first-rate meat dishes.

Sa Caldera €€€ *Bisbe Padre Huix 19; tel: 971 306 416.* House speciality is the *caldereta de llagosta* (a delicious but expensive lobster stew originating in Menorca). Pleasant, discreet setting away from port, behind Santa Cruz church.

San Juan € *Montgrí 8; tel: 971 310 763.* Tiny place where local people mix with tourists, sharing each other's tables. Basic, robust cooking at very reasonable prices.

Sausalito €€€ *Plaça de Sa Riba 5; tel: 971 310 116.* At far end of the quay, the flagship restaurant of Sa Penya quarter, at once elegant and casual. Excellent but expensive Mediterranean cuisine with delicious seafood.

El Vegetariano Cártago € *Punica 8; tel: 971 300 942.* Rare vegetarian restaurant, with good quality vegetable pâtés and salads. Open only weekdays at lunchtime.

Victoria € *Riambau 1; tel: 971 310 622.* Not much point in phoning: just try your luck in this ever-popular, cheerful little place serving traditional food between the port and Vara de Rey.

Sant Antoni

Can Pujol €€ *Badia de Sant Antoni; tel: 971 341 407.* This renowned seafood restaurant specialises in fish in garlic cream sauce but also has a wide range of regional dishes.

Es Pi d'Or €€€ *Carretera Cala Gració; tel: 971 342 872.* Lobster and other seafood specialities from Galicia in an elegant, tranquil setting.

Es Rebost de Can Prats €€ *Carrer de Cervantes 4; tel: 971 346 252.* Traditional Ibenico dishes in a town house restaurant

Grill Magon €€ *Valencia 23, Port des Torrent; tel: 971 340 298.* Nicely prepared grilled steaks, and seafood brought in fresh from nearby fishing harbour.

Mesón Asturiano €€ *Carretera Sant Antoni, Km 12.5; tel: 971 347 531.* Traditional Asturian cooking in pleasant family restaurant. The cider is a speciality of Asturias, in northern Spain.

Mei Ling €€ *Carrer Sant Antoni; tel: 971 343 414.* Widely regarded as the best Chinese restaurant in town.

Pay Pay € *Cala Gració; tel: 971 340 552.* Despite its name, this is an inexpensive Chinese restaurant where the cooking is much better than the view.

Rias Baixas €€€ *Cervantes 14; tel: 971 340 480.* An old restaurant in an attractive new setting – the owner's family home. First-rate beef and seafood in traditional Galician and Asturian styles.

S'Olivar €€€ *Sant Mateu 5; tel: 971 340 010.* Century-old olive tree still grows in centre of restaurant, but main attraction remains the fine classical Spanish and Ibicenco cooking.

Sa Capella €€€ *Capella de Can Bassora, Cami de Cas Ramons; tel: 971 340 057.* Classical Spanish cuisine in elegant setting of an old village church just outside Sant Antoni.

Sa Prensa €€ *Mariano Riquer 9; tel: 971 341 670.* Quiet, clean little restaurant serving traditional Mediterranean food, mainly fish, in a great setting celebrating the island's rich variety of flora.

San Telmo €€ *Sa Drassana 6; tel: 971 310 922.* In a narrow cul-de-sac off Plaça d'Antoni Riquer, away from the port crowds. Classical Spanish and international cuisine.

Zaifiro € *Sant Agustí 118, Port des Torrent; tel: 971 343 903.* Great soups and simple Spanish fare; popular with the local community. Good, cheap set menu.

Santa Eulària

Ama Lur €€€ *Carretera Sant Miquel, Km 23; tel: 971 314 554.* First-class Basque cooking in the attractive setting of a well-renovated traditional *finca* (farmhouse).

Andaluza € *Sant Vicenç 51; tel: 971 339 156.* Succulent tapas-style meals in the old Andaluz tradition. Specialty is *pescaito frito* (fried whitebait).

Ca Na Ribes € *Sant Jaume 67; tel: 971 330 006.* Good fresh fish and grilled steaks, with tables in a courtyard garden.

Can Pau €€€ *Carretera Sant Miquel, Km 8; tel: 971 197 007.* Lovingly restored country house serving authentic Ibicenco dishes, with attentive service and under-stated décor.

Celler Ca'n Pere €€€ *Sant Jaume 73; tel: 971 330 056.* Reputedly the oldest restaurant in Santa Eulària. A traditional wine cellar serving local specialities that include *lechona* (roast suckling pig) and remarkably good wines.

Doña Margarita €€€ *Passeig Marítim; tel: 971 332 200.* Enjoy splendid terrace views over yachting harbour while sampling from a wide-ranging, excellent Mediterranean menu.

Es Timoner €€ *Passeig Marítim; tel: 971 331 723.* Waterside restaurant with small terrace overlooking yachting harbour. Freshest of fresh seafood and excellent Ibicenco lamb, too.

Sant Rafel

El Clodenis €€ *Plaça del Esglèsia; tel: 971 198 545.* 'Le Clos Denis' to its Francophile clientèle. Tasty Provençal cuisine in traditional old country house with garden patio.

Sant Gertrudis

Can Costa € *Plaça del Esglèsia; tel: 971 197 021.* Delicious tapas, sandwiches *(boccadillos)* and slices of ham from those hanging from the ceiling.

Can Pau €€ *Carretera Sant Miquel; tel: 971 197 007.* Outstanding traditional Ibicenco dishes in elegant farmhouse.

La Plaza €€€ *Plaça del Església; tel: 971 197 075.* An enchanting tree-shaded courtyard. Authentic French cuisine with pleasant service.

Sant Josep

Can Domingo de Can Botja €€€ *Carretera Sant Josep, Km 9; tel: 971 800 184.* Combination of Ibicenco and nouvelle cuisine in a handsome country house outside town.

Cana Joana €€€ *Carretera Sant Josep, Km 10; tel: 971 800 158.* Imaginative French and Catalan food in a tranquil, elegantly decorated farmhouse well away from the main road.

Studio Ses Palmeres €€ *Carrer de Valladolid, Port des Torrent; tel: 971 347 654.* Fresh ingredients, lovingly prepared by a notable chef, include carpaccio of tuna.

Victor €€ *Carretera Sant Josep, Km 7.5; tel: 971 800 006.* A large, colourfully decorated garden with an inventive menu (including vegetarian selections).

Sant Joan

Can Gall €€€ *Carretera Sant Joan, Km 11, San Lorenzo; tel: 971 325 055.* A farmhouse restaurant offering classical Ibicenco food and excellent wines. Attentive, friendly staff.

Es Caliu €€ *Carretera Sant Joan, Km 10; tel: 971 325 075.* Rustic garden setting beside a windmill. Authentic Ibicenco cooking.

Es Porrons €€ *Carretera Sant Joan, Km 12; tel: 971 325 151.* Traditional Mediterranean cuisine in farmhouse restaurant with centuries-old carob tree dominating the garden terrace.

Formentera

Aigua €€ *Port de La Savina; tel: 971 323 322.* Popular Italian restaurant right by the harbour.

Bella Vista €€ *Port de La Savina; tel: 971 322 255.* Excellent seafood and fish, but the meat dishes are good, too.

Caminito €€ *Cta Es Pujols–La Savina; tel: 971 328 106.* Delicious steaks served in a cheerful restaurant not far from the beach. Evenings only.

Casa Rafal € *Isidor Macabich, Sant Francesc; tel: 971 322 205.* Bargain prices for simple cooking in a pleasant setting.

Es Moli de Sal €€€ *Platja de ses Illetes, La Savina; tel: 971 136 773.* Seafood dishes served on terrace with superb view of neighbouring island of S'Espalmador and the Ibizan coast.

Es Pla € *Sant Francesc–Cap de Barbaria road, Cala Saona; tel: 971 322 903.* Island cooking and great pizzas served in a pretty garden and frequented mostly by local people.

Recommended Clubs

Ibiza's nightlife can be evanescent, with certain clubs open one season and closed the next. We list here only the half-dozen most solidly established top nightspots. You can also explore the scores of others that come and go with the flashy inconstancy of shooting stars, but which have the special appeal of being often much more outrageous than the island's 'institutions'.

The half-hourly 'Discobus' service (tel: 971 192 456) runs from midnight to 6.30am between Eivissa, Sant Antoni and Santa Eulària and the beach resorts of the main hotels: Platja d'en Bossa, Port des Torrent and Es Canar. Don't go out on the town too early: at many of the clubs, nothing happens before 2am.

All these clubs are expensive: €25–40 per person to enter, plus at least €8 for each drink.

Amnesia *Carretera Sant Antoni, Km 6; tel: 971 191 041.* Huge disco built around an old country house just outside Sant Rafel, a maze of gardens, bars, passageways and mezzanines. Holds 5,000 customers (mostly in their 20s and early 30s), with a casual, non-élitist atmosphere. The crowd is in various states of dress and undress. Famous for introducing the giant foam-bath pool (whipped cream, too).

El Divino *Passeig Marítim, Eivissa Nova; tel: 971 190 176.* On the yachting harbour, linked to Sa Penya quarter by motorboat shuttle. A select, smaller nightclub for a relatively more mature clientele. Magnificent terrace provides bewitching view of town at night. Claims Jack Nicholson and King Juan Carlos among its revellers. Elegant restaurant, where people start eating 'early' – around midnight.

Es Paradis *Salvador Esprui, Sant Antoni; tel: 971 346 600.* Spectacular, with beautiful décor: colonnades festooned with plants and vines. Caters to partygoers in their 30s, at first glance sophisticated, but capable of sustaining music turned up to an ear-splitting decibel level and ultimately willing to be sprayed with water towards the end of the night.

Pacha *Abadordo 33, Eivissa; tel: 971 191 000.* Housed in a remodelled old Ibicenco mansion, this is the island's best-known disco, going strong since the 1970s. The most elegant and fashionable (though by no means the biggest). With four dance floors, countless bars, and a smart restaurant. Specialises in theme evenings and fashion shows.

Privilege *Carretera Sant Antoni, Urbanización Sant Rafel; tel: 971 198 160.* Used to be the legendary Ku, but re-opened in 1994 with this new name. Said to be the biggest club in the world. An outrageous carnival atmosphere, catering in extravagant but playful manner to people of all sexual orientations. Restaurant open 10pm–3am, 15 bars, swimming pool with fountains, gigantic dance floors, capacity up to 8,000.

Space *Platja d'en Bossa; tel: 971 396 793.* For the after-after-hours crowd. Opens its airport road warehouse location about 6am or 7am – when others are closing – and continues well into the afternoon – and sometimes the night. Dancers in cages, with techno music going full blast.

INDEX